Table of Contents

1 Chapter 1: Whispers of the Earth

The forest floor, a tapestry of brown and green, held secrets I yearned to uncover. As a young geology student, my focus had been on the solid, the tangible – rocks, minerals, the very bones of the Earth. Yet, a chance encounter with a decaying log, pulsating with the vibrant orange of a mushroom colony, shifted my perspective irrevocably. I knelt, tracing the delicate gills of a single specimen, captivated by its ephemeral beauty, and a new world unfolded before me, one woven not of stone, but of delicate threads. This encounter ignited a spark, a fascination with the hidden life teeming beneath the surface, a world orchestrated by the silent, yet powerful, forces of mycelia.

My initial exploration revealed a complex web of life, a hidden network connecting the forest in ways I hadn't imagined. The soil, once perceived as mere dirt, transformed into a vibrant ecosystem, a bustling metropolis of fungal hyphae – the microscopic threads that constitute the mycelium. These delicate filaments, invisible to the casual observer, stretched and branched through the earth, forming an intricate latticework that underpinned the forest's vitality. They acted as nature's recyclers, decomposing organic matter, releasing nutrients back into the soil, and facilitating the flow of life through the forest. I learned that this intricate network was not merely a collection of individual organisms, but a dynamic, interconnected system, a living testament to the power of collaboration and symbiosis. The realization that such a complex world existed just beneath my feet was both humbling and exhilarating.

This hidden kingdom, invisible to the untrained eye, became the focus of my growing obsession. Through hours spent observing, reading, and exploring, I began to appreciate the immense diversity and ecological importance of fungi. I discovered that fungi were not just decomposers; they were also crucial partners to plants, forming mycorrhizal relationships that facilitated nutrient exchange and enhanced plant growth. These symbiotic partnerships revealed a level of interconnectedness that challenged my previous understanding of the natural world. The forest wasn't simply a collection of individual organisms competing for resources; it was a complex, interwoven community, with fungi playing a pivotal role in maintaining its delicate balance. The more I delved into this hidden realm, the more I realized how little I knew, and the more profound my fascination became.

I spent countless hours in the field, armed with a hand lens and a growing sense of wonder. Each foray into the forest yielded new discoveries, from the vibrant hues of shelf fungi clinging to fallen logs to the intricate patterns of earthstars nestled amongst the leaf litter. I began to see the forest floor as a vast, unexplored territory, a hidden world teeming with life just waiting to be discovered. The thrill of uncovering a new species, of witnessing the intricate workings of the mycelial network firsthand, fueled my passion and solidified my commitment to understanding this remarkable kingdom. This hands-on exploration was more than just scientific inquiry; it was a journey of discovery, a constant reminder of the Earth's boundless wonders.

As my knowledge deepened, so too did my appreciation for the vital role fungi play in maintaining the health of our planet. They are the architects of decay, the engines of renewal, and the silent partners of the plant kingdom. They are essential to the intricate web of life that sustains us all. And yet, despite their importance, they remain largely overlooked and understudied. This realization fueled my determination to share my fascination with others, to shed light on the hidden world of fungi, and to inspire a greater appreciation for the intricate interconnectedness of life on Earth. My journey into the realm of mycelia had just begun, and I knew it would be a lifelong pursuit, a constant exploration of the whispers of the earth.

The subtle shifts in topography, the composition of the soil, the presence of certain plant species – all became clues in my quest to understand the distribution and behavior of fungal networks. The geological landscape, once my primary focus, now served as a backdrop to a far more intricate and dynamic story, one written in the language of mycelia. I learned to read the subtle signs, the subtle cues that revealed the presence of hidden fungal communities. A slight depression in the ground could indicate the presence of a subterranean fungal network, while the vibrant green of a particular patch of vegetation might suggest a thriving mycorrhizal partnership. The earth, once perceived as solid and unchanging, now pulsed with hidden life, a vibrant ecosystem orchestrated by the silent work of fungi.

My early explorations transformed into a lifelong pursuit, a quest to unravel the mysteries of this hidden kingdom.

1.1   First Encounters

The forest floor crunched beneath my boots, a symphony of decaying leaves and brittle twigs accompanying each step. Sunlight dappled through the canopy, illuminating patches of moss and lichen clinging to the rough bark of ancient trees. I knelt, my geologist's eye scanning the terrain, not for rocks or minerals, but for the subtle signs of a hidden world. A faint, earthy aroma hung in the air, a tantalizing whisper of the life teeming beneath the surface. This was my first real encounter with the captivating realm of mycelia, a world that would forever alter my perspective on the interconnectedness of life.

My initial explorations were clumsy, guided more by intuition than knowledge. I gently probed the soil with my trowel, careful not to disturb the delicate web of life beneath. The top layer yielded fragments of decaying leaves and a tangle of fine roots, but deeper down, a different texture emerged. A gossamer network of white threads, almost invisible to the naked eye, began to reveal itself. These were the hyphae, the building blocks of the vast mycelial network. It felt like uncovering an ancient secret, a hidden language whispered between the trees and the earth.

That first discovery ignited a spark within me. I had spent years studying the geological formations of the Earth, the slow, powerful forces that shape landscapes over millennia. Yet, here beneath my feet, was a different kind of power, a subtle yet pervasive force that connected the living world in ways I had never imagined.

The intricate web of hyphae extended far beyond my small excavation, a vast underground network weaving its way through the forest. It was a biological internet, connecting trees and other plants, facilitating communication and resource sharing on a scale I found utterly fascinating.

Later encounters brought me face-to-face with the sheer diversity of fungal forms. A fallen log, seemingly lifeless, pulsed with activity upon closer inspection. Shelves of vibrant orange bracket fungi clung to its sides, their textured surfaces a testament to the relentless work of decomposition. Delicate oyster mushrooms, their caps resembling ethereal fans, emerged from crevices in the bark. Each species, a unique expression of the fungal kingdom, played a specific role in the intricate dance of life and decay.

One particularly memorable encounter involved a patch of bright red Amanita muscaria, their iconic caps dotted with white warts. These striking fungi, while beautiful, held a potent secret within their tissues. Their toxicity served as a reminder of the complex chemical interactions taking place within the fungal world, a world of both healing and harm. This experience underscored the importance of careful observation and identification, a crucial skill for any budding mycologist.

As I continued my explorations, I learned to recognize the subtle signs of mycelial presence. The appearance of certain plant communities, the texture of the soil, even the faint scent of the air could offer clues to the hidden networks below. Each encounter deepened my appreciation for the crucial role fungi play in maintaining the health and balance of ecosystems. They were the recyclers, the decomposers, the connectors, silently orchestrating the flow of nutrients and energy through the forest.

My initial foray into the world of mycelia was a transformative experience. It shifted my focus from the grand geological narratives of the Earth to the intricate biological stories unfolding beneath my feet. The forest floor, once a simple collection of leaves and soil, became a portal to a hidden world of unimaginable complexity and beauty. It was the beginning of a lifelong journey of discovery, a journey that continues to inspire and amaze me to this day. The whispers of the earth, once faint and elusive, had become a clear and compelling call, drawing me deeper into the mesmerizing melody of mycelia. The intricate tapestry of fungal life, woven into the very fabric of the forest, was a constant reminder of the interconnectedness of all living things, a lesson I would carry with me throughout my explorations. This initial fascination, this spark of curiosity, would evolve into a deep passion, driving me to unravel the mysteries of this hidden kingdom and share its wonders with the world.

1.2   The Mycelial Web

Imagine the earth beneath our feet not as solid, inert matter, but as a vibrant, interconnected web of life. This is the realm of the mycelium, the hidden network of fungal filaments that weaves its way through soil and rock, connecting plants and ecosystems in ways we are only beginning to understand. Mycelia are the unseen architects of our world, shaping landscapes, driving nutrient cycles, and playing a vital role in the delicate balance of nature. They exist as a hidden infrastructure, a living internet beneath our feet, pulsing with information and energy.

This network, often invisible to the naked eye, is a complex tapestry of interconnected hyphae, thread-like structures that explore and colonize their environment. These hyphae branch and fuse, creating a vast, decentralized system that can extend for miles beneath the forest floor. Consider a single teaspoon of healthy soil; it can contain miles of these microscopic fungal highways. This intricate network is not merely a physical structure, but a dynamic and responsive organism. It reacts to changes in moisture, temperature, and nutrient availability, constantly adapting and reshaping itself to optimize its growth and survival. This plasticity allows the mycelium to thrive in a wide range of environments, from the deepest forests to the harshest deserts.

The implications of this interconnectedness are profound. Through the mycelial web, nutrients and resources are shared between plants, creating a complex system of interdependence. Trees, for instance, can communicate and support each other through these fungal networks, sending nutrients to seedlings struggling in the shade or warning of impending insect attacks. This intricate communication system highlights the critical role of fungi in maintaining the health and resilience of forest ecosystems. It's a silent, subterranean language, a whisper of the earth that reveals the deep interconnectedness of life.

Furthermore, the mycelium plays a crucial role in decomposition, breaking down organic matter and returning essential nutrients to the soil. This process is fundamental to the cycling of life, ensuring that the building blocks of life are continuously recycled and made available for new growth. Without the tireless work of these fungal decomposers, our world would be choked with dead plant matter, and the vital flow of nutrients would grind to a halt. They are the earth's recyclers, the engines of renewal that drive the continuous cycle of birth, death, and rebirth.

As a field geologist, I've witnessed firsthand the intricate beauty and remarkable power of the mycelial web. I've seen it weaving through layers of rock and soil, binding together different strata and influencing the very structure of the landscape. I've traced its delicate threads through ancient forests, marveling at its ability to connect vast ecosystems and orchestrate the flow of life. These experiences have instilled in me a deep respect for the hidden world beneath our feet, a world that is often overlooked but is essential to the health and well-being of our planet.

From the perspective of a geologist, understanding the mycelial network offers a new lens through which to view the Earth's processes. It highlights the interconnectedness of the geological and biological realms, demonstrating how the physical structure of the Earth influences the distribution and development of life, and how life, in turn, shapes the very earth beneath our feet. It's a dynamic interplay, a constant dance between the living and the non-living.

Exploring the microscopic world of the mycelium reveals a hidden universe of intricate structures and complex interactions. The hyphal tips, constantly exploring and expanding, are the pioneers of this subterranean frontier, probing and adapting to the ever-changing conditions of their environment. Their growth and branching patterns, influenced by factors such as nutrient availability and moisture gradients, create a constantly shifting landscape within the soil.

Understanding the structure and function of the mycelial web is crucial for comprehending the intricate workings of our planet's ecosystems. It reveals the vital role of fungi in maintaining soil health, facilitating nutrient cycling, and supporting the growth and resilience of plant communities. This hidden network, often overlooked, is a fundamental component of the Earth's life support system, a silent partner in the intricate dance of life. It's a testament to the interconnectedness of all living things, a reminder that even the smallest and most hidden organisms play a vital role in the grand symphony of nature.

The exploration of the mycelial web requires careful observation and meticulous fieldwork. It involves digging into the soil, carefully examining root systems, and using specialized techniques to visualize the intricate network of fungal hyphae. This hands-on approach allows us to gain a deeper understanding of the complex interactions between fungi, plants, and the environment. It's a process of discovery, a journey into the hidden world beneath our feet.

By delving into this subterranean realm, we uncover a hidden world of remarkable complexity and beauty. We begin to appreciate the intricate connections that bind together the different components of our ecosystems, and we gain a deeper understanding of the vital role that fungi play in maintaining the health and balance of our planet. It's a journey of exploration, a quest to unravel the mysteries of the mycelial web and unlock the secrets of the earth beneath our feet. It is a journey that reveals the profound interconnectedness of life and the vital role of the unseen world in shaping our planet.

1.3 A Hidden World

The forest floor, a tapestry of brown and green, concealed a universe I was only beginning to comprehend. Beneath the decaying leaves, a silent, intricate network pulsed with life – the mycelium. Not roots, not plants, but something altogether different, a hidden kingdom orchestrating the flow of nutrients and information through the forest. This was a world of delicate threads, of hyphal tips exploring the microscopic spaces between soil particles, a world of chemical signals and symbiotic partnerships, a world that held the forest together. My geologist's eye, trained to see patterns in rock formations and landscapes, was now captivated by the intricate architecture of this subterranean realm.

I knelt, gently brushing aside the leaf litter to reveal the fine, white filaments. They reminded me of the branching veins of quartz in a granite outcrop, or the dendritic patterns etched into a canyon wall by flowing water. These delicate strands weren't just static structures; they were dynamic, constantly growing, exploring, and responding to the environment. This wasn't just a network; it was a living, breathing entity. I thought of the vast mycelial mats discovered beneath ancient forests, stretching for kilometers, connecting trees of different species, a silent communication network operating beneath our feet. The realization of this vast interconnectedness, this hidden world driving the forest ecosystem, filled me with a sense of wonder.

My initial explorations involved careful excavation. Using a trowel and a soft brush, I would painstakingly uncover sections of the mycelial network, marveling at its complexity. I learned to differentiate between the rhizomorphs, thick cord-like structures that transported nutrients over long distances, and the finer, more delicate hyphae responsible for absorbing resources from the surrounding soil. I discovered the sclerotia, hardened, compact masses of mycelium that served as nutrient stores and survival structures during harsh conditions. Each discovery deepened my fascination with this hidden world.

With a hand lens, I could observe the intricate details of the hyphae, the individual cells joined end-to-end, forming the building blocks of the mycelial network. I began to understand the crucial role of these microscopic structures in decomposing organic matter, releasing nutrients back into the soil, and facilitating the growth of plants. It was a humbling realization: this seemingly insignificant network was a fundamental driver of life in the forest.

As I continued my explorations, I began to appreciate the sheer diversity of fungal forms. From the delicate, fan-like structures of oyster mushrooms to the robust, earthy caps of boletes, the fruiting bodies of fungi offered a glimpse into the hidden world below. Each species had its own unique morphology, its own preferred habitat, and its own role to play in the ecosystem. I learned to identify different species based on their macroscopic features – the shape and color of the cap, the presence or absence of gills or pores, the texture of the stem.

But the true magic lay in understanding the connections, the intricate relationships between the fungi and their environment. The mycorrhizal associations, the symbiotic partnerships between fungi and plant roots, were a prime example of this interdependence. I learned how the fungal hyphae extended the reach of plant roots, allowing them to access water and nutrients they wouldn't otherwise be able to reach. In return, the plants provided the fungi with sugars produced through photosynthesis. This mutualistic relationship, hidden beneath the surface, was the foundation of the forest ecosystem.

Further investigation revealed the role of fungi in nutrient cycling. I observed how different species specialized in decomposing different types of organic matter – wood, leaves, even animal carcasses. This process of decomposition released essential nutrients back into the soil, making them available for plants and other organisms. The fungi were the recyclers of the forest, the engines of renewal.

The more I learned, the more I realized how much remained unknown. The hidden world of mycelia was vast and complex, a frontier of scientific discovery. My journey had just begun, and I was eager to continue exploring the intricate melodies of this fascinating kingdom. The forest floor, once a familiar landscape, had become a portal to a world of wonder.

2 Chapter 2: Beneath the Surface

The trowel bites into the earth, a cool, damp scent rising from the freshly turned soil. This isn't just dirt; it's a universe unto itself, a hidden world teeming with life. My work as a field geologist often takes me below the surface, beyond the familiar landscapes of rock and sediment, into the realm of the unseen. Here, among the intricate lattices of roots and the myriad microorganisms, lies the focus of my fascination: the mycelium. It's a realm where geological forces and fungal life intertwine in a delicate dance.

The underlying geology of an area dramatically influences the nature of the mycelial networks that thrive within it. Soil composition, a direct product of the parent rock material, dictates the availability of essential nutrients for fungal growth. A granite-derived soil, for instance, will be acidic and nutrient-poor, favoring certain acid-tolerant fungal species. Conversely, a soil derived from limestone will be alkaline and richer in minerals, supporting a different fungal community altogether. The texture of the soil, influenced by the size and shape of the weathered rock particles, impacts drainage and aeration, further shaping the environment for mycelial growth. Think of the difference between a dense clay and a loose, sandy soil: one restricts water movement and oxygen diffusion, while the other promotes it, leading to distinct fungal populations.

The very structure of the bedrock itself plays a crucial role in guiding the development of subterranean mycelial networks. Fractures and fissures within the rock, created by tectonic forces or weathering processes, act as conduits for fungal hyphae. These microscopic threads can penetrate deep into the rock matrix, accessing moisture and minerals unavailable to surface organisms. I've encountered stunning examples of this in my fieldwork, uncovering fungal networks tracing the intricate patterns of fractures in exposed rock faces. These networks, invisible from above, highlight the hidden pathways that fungi exploit to colonize the subterranean realm. The dip and strike of rock strata, those fundamental geological measurements describing the orientation of rock layers, also influence water flow and drainage patterns, indirectly impacting mycelial distribution.

Water, the lifeblood of all living things, exerts a profound influence on fungal growth. The presence of groundwater, its depth, and its movement through the subsurface are critical factors in shaping the distribution and abundance of mycelia. Areas with high water tables tend to favor specific types of fungi adapted to waterlogged conditions, while drier regions support drought-tolerant species. I recall a particular field study in a riparian zone, a transitional area between land and a river. Here, the fluctuating water table created a dynamic environment, supporting a remarkably diverse array of fungal species, each adapted to a specific moisture regime within the soil profile.

Understanding the relationship between geology and mycelial growth requires careful observation and meticulous fieldwork. I often employ techniques borrowed from geological surveys, adapting them to the study of fungal networks. Soil sampling, for instance, allows me to analyze the physical and chemical properties of the soil, revealing the nutrient content and other factors influencing fungal growth. Ground-penetrating radar, a tool commonly used in geophysical exploration, can be employed to visualize the subsurface structure and identify potential pathways for mycelial growth along fractures and bedding planes.

Careful excavation and exposure of soil profiles reveal the intricate layering of the subsurface and the distribution of fungal communities within these layers. I meticulously document these profiles, noting the changes in soil texture, color, and the presence of fungal hyphae at different depths. Microscopic analysis of soil samples provides further insights into the diversity of fungal species present. Each field site presents a unique puzzle, challenging me to decipher the complex interplay of geological factors and fungal life.

This work isn't just about collecting data; it's about unraveling a story. The story of how the Earth, through its geological formations and processes, shapes the hidden world of mycelia. It's a story that unfolds beneath our feet, a silent symphony of interactions between rock, soil, water, and the intricate web of fungal life. And it's a story that I, as a field geologist, am privileged to explore.

2.1 Digging Deeper

The trowel scrapes against a layer of shale, a subtle shift in the earth's texture a tell-tale sign. I pause, brush away loose particles, and reveal a network of fine, white threads clinging to the underside of the rock. This isn't just any rock fragment; it's a microhabitat, a miniature world shaped by the relentless work of fungal hyphae. These delicate filaments, the building blocks of mycelium, are the hidden architects of our subterranean landscapes. They penetrate crevices, bind soil particles, and orchestrate the slow, steady decomposition of organic matter. Their presence, often invisible to the untrained eye, speaks volumes about the geological history and ecological dynamics of a place.

My fieldwork in the semi-arid regions of Spain has revealed a fascinating interplay between fungal colonization and rock weathering. The gypsum-rich soils of these landscapes offer a unique challenge for life, characterized by high salinity and low water retention. Yet, within these seemingly hostile conditions, fungi thrive. I've observed how specific fungal species etch microscopic channels into gypsum crystals, accelerating their dissolution and contributing to the formation of distinctive soil structures. This biological weathering, a silent dialogue between the lithosphere and the biosphere, underscores the power of these tiny organisms to shape the very foundations of our planet.

The depth at which mycelial networks penetrate the earth varies dramatically depending on factors such as soil type, moisture content, and nutrient availability. In the loose, sandy soils of coastal dunes, for instance, I've found extensive mats of mycelium just a few centimeters below the surface, interwoven with the roots of dune grasses. These fungal networks act as a living glue, stabilizing the shifting sands and creating a hospitable environment for plant life. Contrastingly, in dense clay soils, fungal hyphae must navigate a much more compact and resistant medium. Their progress is slower, more deliberate, and often concentrated along fissures and root channels. Here, the mycelium becomes a subterranean explorer, charting pathways through the earth's hidden depths.

Further down, in the cool, dark realm of bedrock, fungal activity takes on a different character. Here, the focus shifts from decomposition to the slow, relentless process of mineral weathering. Endolithic fungi, specialized species adapted to life within rock pores, secrete organic acids that dissolve minerals, extracting essential nutrients and contributing to the gradual breakdown of even the hardest substrates. This hidden alchemy, occurring over geological timescales, has played a pivotal role in shaping the Earth's crust and creating the conditions for life as we know it.

Studying these subterranean ecosystems requires a multidisciplinary approach. My geological background, combined with a growing understanding of fungal ecology, allows me to appreciate the complex interplay between the biotic and abiotic worlds. Examining thin sections of rock under a microscope reveals the intricate patterns of fungal colonization, showcasing the intimate relationship between these organisms and their mineral substrates. Chemical analysis of soil samples provides insights into the nutrient cycling processes mediated by fungal activity. And meticulous field observations, from carefully excavated soil profiles to the subtle changes in vegetation patterns, offer clues to the hidden workings of the mycelial network.

One particularly memorable excavation took place in the foothills of the Sierra Nevada mountains. While investigating a series of ancient limestone caves, I discovered a network of biofilms coating the cave walls. These biofilms, composed of bacteria, algae, and fungi, were actively dissolving the limestone, creating intricate patterns of erosion. The fungi, acting as key players in this microbial community, secreted enzymes that broke down the calcium carbonate matrix of the rock. This process, known as biokarst, contributes to the formation of cave systems and shapes the subterranean drainage patterns of entire landscapes.

My experiences in the field have instilled in me a profound respect for the hidden power of fungi. These often-overlooked organisms play a crucial role in shaping the Earth's surface, driving nutrient cycles, and supporting the vast web of life. As I continue my exploration of the mycelial melody, I am constantly reminded of the intricate connections that bind the geological and biological realms, and the importance of preserving these fragile subterranean ecosystems. Each dig, each sample, each microscopic observation reveals a new layer of complexity, deepening my appreciation for the hidden wonders that lie beneath our feet. The intricate network, pulsating with life, reveals its secrets to those who are patient enough to listen. The melody of mycelia, once a whisper, becomes a symphony.

2.2   Unearthing Secrets

The trowel scrapes against a layer of compressed clay, a subtle shift in texture hinting at a change in the earth's story. I kneel, brushing loose soil away to reveal the pale threads weaving through the dark substrate. This is what I came for, the hidden architecture of the underground, the whispers of millennia etched in the delicate tracery of mycelia. Each thread, a hypha, stretches and branches, an intricate network mapping the flow of nutrients, the ebb and flow of life and decay within this hidden realm. This particular site, nestled at the base of a weathered limestone cliff, promises a unique glimpse into the relationship between geology and fungal colonization.

Limestone, a sedimentary rock formed from ancient marine organisms, presents a unique environment for fungal growth. Its porous nature allows for water retention, crucial for fungal life, while the slow dissolution of calcium carbonate releases minerals essential for hyphal development. I carefully extract a small block of soil and rock, noting the distinct stratification. Bands of varying color and texture reveal past environmental conditions, each layer a time capsule preserving the history of this microcosm. Within these layers, the mycelial network adapts and responds, its growth patterns reflecting the subtle shifts in pH, moisture, and nutrient availability.

Here, within a band of reddish-brown clay, the mycelia are densely packed, forming a thick mat. This suggests a period of increased organic matter deposition, perhaps from leaf litter accumulating at the base of the cliff. The clay itself provides a stable substrate, holding moisture and allowing the hyphae to thrive. In contrast, the adjacent layer, a pale yellow sand, shows a sparser network. This sandy layer, more porous and less nutrient-rich, likely posed a greater challenge for fungal colonization, resulting in a more fragmented network. These variations, seemingly insignificant, paint a vivid picture of the dynamic interplay between geology and fungal life, revealing how the earth's structure shapes the hidden world beneath our feet. I carefully collect samples from each layer, placing them in sterile bags for later analysis. Back in the lab, I will use microscopy to identify the specific fungal species present and analyze their isotopic signatures. These analyses will provide further clues about the age and origin of the fungal community and how it has adapted to the unique geological conditions of this site. By studying the isotopic composition of the fungal tissues, we can trace the flow of nutrients within the ecosystem, understanding how fungi contribute to the cycling of carbon and other essential elements.

The connection between geology and fungal growth extends beyond the immediate substrate. The slope of the land, the direction of water flow, even the presence of nearby trees, all influence the distribution and diversity of fungal communities. For example, on the north-facing slope of the cliff, where conditions are cooler and moister, I find a different suite of fungal species compared to the sun-baked south-facing slope. This highlights the importance of considering the broader landscape when studying fungal ecology. The geological context provides the framework, while local environmental factors fine-tune the composition of the fungal community.

My work here, piecing together the clues hidden within the soil and rock, allows me to reconstruct the past, to understand the intricate interplay of forces that have shaped this landscape over millennia. Each fragment of mycelium, each layer of sediment, tells a story. And it's through these stories, whispered by the earth itself, that we gain a deeper appreciation for the interconnectedness of life and the vital role that fungi play in the planet's grand symphony. This quiet, unseen world holds the key to understanding the Earth's past and, perhaps, its future. The whispers of the mycelia guide us, revealing the secrets of the earth, one layer at a time. As I pack up my tools, the setting sun casting long shadows across the cliff face, I feel a sense of awe and gratitude for the opportunity to witness this hidden world and to contribute to our understanding of its intricate beauty and profound importance. The earth holds its secrets close, but with patience and careful observation, we can begin to unearth them, revealing the symphony of life beneath our feet.

3 Chapter 3: The Fungal Symphony

The fungal world isn't a silent, static landscape. It's a vibrant, dynamic orchestra, with each species playing a unique part in a grand, interconnected symphony. Consider the wood-decay fungi, the tireless decomposers. These organisms, often unseen, diligently break down fallen trees, leaf litter, and other organic matter, releasing essential nutrients back into the soil. Without their tireless work, forests would become choked with debris, and the vital cycle of nutrient flow would grind to a halt. They are the unseen conductors, orchestrating the flow of life's essential elements.

This decomposition process, while seemingly simple, is a complex biochemical ballet. Different species specialize in breaking down different components of wood, like lignin and cellulose. Some fungi employ powerful enzymes to penetrate the tough outer layers of wood, while others thrive on the partially decomposed material left behind. This division of labor ensures efficient and complete decomposition, maximizing nutrient recycling. The fascinating aspect of this decomposition process is its quiet elegance, a subtle yet powerful force shaping the forest ecosystem.

Beyond the decomposers, a multitude of other fungal species contribute to the symphony of the soil. Mycorrhizal fungi, for instance, form intimate partnerships with plant roots. These fungi extend the reach of the plant's root system, effectively increasing its access to water and nutrients. In return, the plant provides the fungus with sugars produced through photosynthesis. This symbiotic relationship, a delicate dance of give and take, benefits both partners and strengthens the entire ecosystem. It underscores the interconnectedness of life in the soil, a reminder that even seemingly independent organisms often rely on each other for survival.

The rhythm of life in the fungal kingdom is intimately tied to the seasons. Temperature, moisture, and the availability of nutrients all influence fungal growth and reproduction. During the warm, damp months, fungal activity peaks, with mycelia spreading rapidly and fruiting bodies emerging to release spores. As winter approaches, many fungi enter a dormant state, conserving energy until favorable conditions return. This cyclical pattern of growth and dormancy, a response to the changing environment, contributes to the overall stability of the ecosystem.

The interplay between decay and renewal is central to the fungal symphony. As fungi decompose organic matter, they release nutrients that fuel new growth. This continuous cycle of breakdown and regeneration is the engine that drives life in forests and other ecosystems. It's a testament to the interconnectedness of life and death, where the end of one organism provides the foundation for the next. This intricate dance of life and death is a fundamental principle of ecology, highlighting the crucial role fungi play in maintaining balance.

Mycorrhizal networks, often described as the "wood wide web," further amplify this interconnectedness. These vast underground networks connect the roots of different plants, allowing them to communicate and share resources. Through these fungal pathways, trees can transfer nutrients to seedlings struggling in the shade, or even warn each other of impending threats like insect attacks. This complex communication system, facilitated by fungal networks, reveals the surprising sophistication of plant communities.

The diversity within the fungal kingdom is truly astounding. From the microscopic yeasts used in baking and brewing to the macroscopic mushrooms that grace our forests, fungi exhibit a remarkable range of forms and functions. Each species has its own unique niche within the ecosystem, contributing to the overall harmony of the fungal symphony. This vast diversity, a testament to the evolutionary success of fungi, provides a rich tapestry of ecological interactions.

Understanding the fungal symphony requires careful observation and a willingness to delve beneath the surface. By studying the interactions between different fungal species, their relationship with the environment, and their impact on other organisms, we can gain a deeper appreciation for the complex web of life that sustains our planet. This exploration, a journey into the hidden world of fungi, offers a unique perspective on the interconnectedness of all living things.

The beauty of the fungal symphony lies in its subtle complexity. It's a reminder that even the smallest organisms play vital roles in the grand scheme of life. By appreciating the intricate workings of this hidden world, we gain a deeper understanding of the interconnectedness of nature and the importance of preserving its delicate balance. This appreciation, a testament to the wonders of the natural world, inspires us to protect and cherish the delicate balance of our planet.

The study of fungi is a journey of continuous discovery. With each new species identified and each new interaction revealed, our understanding of the fungal symphony deepens. This ongoing exploration, a testament to the vastness of the natural world, offers endless opportunities for learning and wonder. The fungal world, a realm of hidden wonders, awaits those who dare to explore its depths.

3.1   Nature's Conductors

Fungi, often relegated to the shadowy corners of the natural world, are in reality dynamic orchestrators of life, death, and renewal. They are the conductors of nature's symphony, directing the flow of nutrients and energy through the ecosystem. Consider the intricate web of hyphae, the thread-like filaments that comprise the mycelium. These delicate strands, invisible to the casual observer, weave through the soil, binding together the earth and facilitating communication between plants. This interconnectedness is not simply structural; it represents a complex chemical dialogue, a constant exchange of vital resources and information.

Through their extensive mycelial networks, fungi decompose organic matter, breaking down complex molecules and returning essential nutrients to the soil. This process, often perceived as decay, is in fact a fundamental act of creation. It is through decomposition that the building blocks of life are made available for new growth. Imagine a forest floor carpeted with fallen leaves. Without the diligent work of fungi, these leaves would accumulate, smothering the soil and preventing the regeneration of the forest.

The role of fungi as decomposers is just one facet of their multifaceted contribution to ecosystem health. Consider mycorrhizal fungi, which form symbiotic relationships with plant roots. These fungi extend the reach of plant root systems, allowing them to access nutrients and water they would otherwise be unable to reach. In return, the plants provide the fungi with sugars produced through photosynthesis. This mutually beneficial partnership underscores the intricate web of interdependence that characterizes the natural world. It is a delicate balance, a testament to the power of cooperation.

Further exploration of the fungal kingdom reveals a staggering diversity of species, each with its own unique characteristics and ecological role. From the ubiquitous button mushroom to the bioluminescent fungi that glow in the dark, the fungal world is brimming with surprising adaptations. Some fungi are essential for the production of certain foods and medicines, while others play a crucial role in nutrient cycling and soil formation. This diversity reflects the remarkable adaptability of fungi, their ability to thrive in a wide range of environments.

The study of fungal networks requires a keen eye for detail and a deep understanding of ecological processes. As a field geologist, I have spent countless hours observing the subtle signs of fungal activity, from the fruiting bodies that emerge above ground to the intricate patterns of mycelial growth revealed through careful excavation. Each foray into the field yields new insights into the hidden world of fungi, revealing the complex interplay between geology, ecology, and the fungal kingdom. This meticulous observation, combined with scientific analysis, allows us to unravel the secrets of these remarkable organisms.

My own fascination with fungi began early in my career, during a geological survey in the remote mountains. While examining a rock outcrop, I noticed a delicate network of white filaments clinging to the underside of a loose stone. Intrigued, I carefully removed the stone, revealing a thriving community of fungi. This chance encounter sparked a lifelong passion for mycology, leading me down a path of discovery that has enriched my understanding of the natural world in countless ways. It was a pivotal moment, a reminder of the hidden wonders that await those who take the time to observe.

The interconnectedness of the natural world is perhaps nowhere more evident than in the realm of fungi. These often-overlooked organisms play a vital role in maintaining ecological balance, driving nutrient cycles, and supporting the growth of plant life. As we continue to explore the intricate web of life on Earth, it is essential that we recognize the critical importance of fungi and work to protect their habitats. Their survival is inextricably linked to our own, a testament to the interconnectedness of all living things. By understanding and appreciating the role of fungi as nature's conductors, we can gain a deeper appreciation for the delicate symphony of life that surrounds us. This understanding is not just scientific knowledge; it is a profound realization of our place within the grand tapestry of existence. It's a call to stewardship, a responsibility to protect the intricate web of life that sustains us all. The future of our planet depends on it.

3.2 A Chorus of Species

The fungal kingdom bursts with an astounding array of species, each playing a unique role in the intricate web of life beneath our feet. From the microscopic yeasts used in baking to the towering mushrooms that grace our forests, the diversity within this kingdom is breathtaking. Consider the unassuming yet crucial role of decomposer fungi. These organisms, often hidden amongst leaf litter or within decaying wood, are nature's recyclers. They break down complex organic matter, releasing essential nutrients back into the soil, making them available for plants and other organisms. Without these tireless workers, the cycle of life would grind to a halt.

Then there are the pathogenic fungi, a group often perceived negatively due to their role in causing diseases in plants and animals. Yet, even these organisms play a vital role in ecosystem dynamics. They act as a natural check on populations, preventing unchecked growth and promoting biodiversity. Studying their interactions reveals fascinating insights into the complex relationships within ecological communities. Think of the Dutch elm disease, caused by a fungus carried by bark beetles. While devastating to elm populations, it has reshaped the landscape and created opportunities for other tree species to thrive. This intricate dance of life and death highlights the interconnectedness of all species.

Consider the remarkable symbiotic relationships formed by mycorrhizal fungi. These fungi form intimate connections with plant roots, creating a network of exchange. The fungal hyphae, thread-like filaments, extend the reach of the plant's root system, enhancing its ability to absorb water and nutrients. In return, the plant provides the fungus with sugars produced through photosynthesis. This mutually beneficial partnership is crucial for the health and resilience of many ecosystems, particularly in nutrient-poor environments. Orchid seeds, for instance, rely entirely on mycorrhizal fungi for germination and early development, showcasing the depth of this symbiotic relationship.

Lichens, another fascinating example of symbiotic partnership, represent a complex fusion of fungi and algae or cyanobacteria. The fungus provides structure and protection, while the algal partner performs photosynthesis, providing food for the combined organism. Lichens are incredibly adaptable, colonizing diverse habitats from bare rock to tree bark. They play a crucial role in soil formation and contribute significantly to the biodiversity of many ecosystems, particularly in harsh environments. Their presence often indicates a healthy and undisturbed environment, serving as a bioindicator of air quality.

Exploring the diversity of fungal species requires an understanding of their morphology, their physical form and structure. Macroscopic fungi, those visible to the naked eye, exhibit an impressive array of shapes, sizes, and colors. From the delicate gills of a mushroom to the intricate folds of a morel, these structures reflect the reproductive strategies of the fungi. Microscopic fungi, on the other hand, require specialized equipment for observation. Their intricate structures and diverse forms are equally fascinating, revealing a hidden world of complexity. Observing these microscopic marvels under a microscope opens up a whole new dimension of fungal diversity.

Beyond morphology, understanding the physiological processes of fungi is essential. How do they obtain nutrients? How do they reproduce? How do they interact with their environment? These questions drive research into the fascinating world of fungal physiology. Consider the role of enzymes in fungal decomposition. These complex proteins break down organic matter, enabling fungi to access essential nutrients. The study of these enzymes has far-reaching implications, from biotechnology to bioremediation. Understanding how fungi break down complex materials holds immense potential for developing sustainable solutions for waste management and environmental cleanup.

The study of fungal genetics provides another layer of understanding, allowing us to explore the evolutionary history and relationships between different species. By analyzing fungal DNA, we can trace their lineage and uncover the evolutionary forces that have shaped their diversity. This information is crucial for understanding the complex web of life on Earth and for developing strategies for conservation and sustainable management of fungal resources. For example, genetic analysis can reveal the origins of pathogenic fungi, helping us to understand how they evolve and adapt to new environments.

Finally, the ecological roles of fungi extend far beyond decomposition and symbiosis. They influence nutrient cycling, soil structure, and even the climate. They interact with a wide range of organisms, playing critical roles in food webs and ecosystem stability. As we continue to explore the fungal kingdom, we are constantly discovering new and fascinating aspects of their biology and ecology. The study of fungi is a journey of discovery, uncovering the hidden melodies of the mycelial world and revealing the profound impact these organisms have on our planet.

3.3   The Rhythm of Life

The pulse of the forest floor, often unseen, vibrates with a rhythm dictated by decay and renewal. This isn't a morbid cycle, but rather a transformative dance. Fallen leaves, crumbling branches, and the remnants of past life become the substrate for future growth, orchestrated by the tireless work of fungal decomposers. Consider the intricate web of hyphae that penetrate a decaying log, breaking down complex organic molecules into simpler forms. These liberated nutrients then become available for other organisms, fueling the continuous cycle of life, death, and rebirth. This process, driven by fungal activity, is fundamental to the health and vitality of the forest ecosystem.

The rhythm extends beyond decomposition, influencing the very structure and stability of the soil. Fungal hyphae act as tiny anchors, binding soil particles together and creating a porous network that improves water infiltration and aeration. This intricate architecture allows for better nutrient cycling and provides a stable habitat for a myriad of soil-dwelling organisms. Imagine the delicate balance maintained by this unseen network, a hidden world supporting the visible grandeur of the forest above. The stability provided by the fungal mycelium is crucial for preventing erosion and maintaining the overall health of the land.

This rhythmic interplay between decay and renewal manifests itself in various temporal scales. The rapid decomposition of a leaf litter layer contributes to short-term nutrient cycling, while the slow decay of a fallen tree can influence forest dynamics for decades. Observe the subtle changes in the forest floor throughout the seasons. The flush of fungal fruiting bodies after a rain, the gradual softening of fallen wood, the emergence of new seedlings amidst the decaying leaves—all these are expressions of the continuous cycle driven by fungal activity. This temporal diversity creates a mosaic of habitats, supporting a wide array of species with different life histories and ecological roles.

Furthermore, the rhythm of decay and renewal is intimately connected to the larger cycles of the earth's systems. The carbon cycle, for instance, relies heavily on fungal decomposition to release carbon dioxide back into the atmosphere. This release, in turn, influences global climate patterns and contributes to the overall balance of the planet's carbon budget. The intricate relationship between fungal activity and global processes highlights the interconnectedness of all living things and the crucial role that fungi play in regulating Earth's systems.

Consider the specific example of a white-rot fungus colonizing a dead tree. These fungi possess unique enzymes that can break down lignin, a complex polymer that gives wood its rigidity. This decomposition process not only releases nutrients back into the ecosystem but also contributes to the formation of humus, a dark, organic material that enriches the soil and improves its water-holding capacity. The transformation of a rigid tree trunk into fertile soil exemplifies the power of fungal decomposition and its role in shaping the landscape.

The cyclical nature of fungal activity also extends to the relationship between different species. Certain fungi are specialized decomposers of specific organic materials, while others rely on the byproducts of these primary decomposers. This intricate web of interactions creates a complex food web within the soil, supporting a vast diversity of organisms, from microscopic bacteria to larger invertebrates. The interdependence of these organisms highlights the importance of biodiversity in maintaining a healthy and resilient ecosystem.

Understanding the rhythm of decay and renewal is crucial for appreciating the ecological significance of fungi. They are not merely agents of decomposition but rather essential players in the intricate symphony of life on Earth. Their tireless work ensures the continuous flow of nutrients, the stability of the soil, and the overall health of our planet's ecosystems. By recognizing and respecting the rhythm of the fungal world, we can gain a deeper understanding of the interconnectedness of all living things and the importance of conserving this vital component of our natural world. The next time you walk through a forest, take a moment to consider the hidden world beneath your feet, where the tireless work of fungi orchestrates the continuous cycle of life, death, and rebirth.

3.4   Decay and Renewal

The ceaseless cycle of decay and renewal is arguably the most fundamental contribution fungi make to the planet's health. Consider the forest floor, a tapestry woven with fallen leaves, decaying branches, and the remnants of life. Without the tireless work of fungal decomposers, this organic debris would accumulate relentlessly, smothering the very life it once supported. Fungi, with their specialized enzymes, break down complex organic molecules like lignin and cellulose, unlocking nutrients locked within dead plant matter. These liberated nutrients then become available to other organisms, fueling new growth and perpetuating the cycle of life. This process, far from being morbid, is a vibrant expression of transformation and rebirth. It is a symphony of decay orchestrated by a hidden conductor – the mycelium.

This decomposition process isn't uniform. The rate of decay is influenced by a complex interplay of factors, including temperature, moisture levels, the type of organic matter, and the specific fungal species involved. In cooler, drier environments, decomposition proceeds more slowly, while warm, humid conditions accelerate the process. Different fungi specialize in breaking down different substrates. Some excel at degrading wood, others prefer leaf litter, and still others thrive on the remains of animals. This specialization contributes to the biodiversity of fungal communities and ensures efficient recycling of various organic materials within an ecosystem. This intricate interplay highlights the interconnectedness of the natural world.

Fungal decomposition has profound implications for soil formation and structure. As fungi break down organic matter, they release humic substances, complex organic molecules that contribute to soil fertility and water retention. These substances bind soil particles together, improving soil structure and creating a more hospitable environment for plant roots. The extensive network of mycelium itself also plays a crucial role in soil stability, binding soil aggregates together and preventing erosion. The very architecture of healthy soil is, in large part, a testament to the tireless work of fungal networks. They are the unseen architects of the earth beneath our feet.

Beyond the breakdown of organic matter, fungi participate in another crucial aspect of renewal: nutrient cycling. As fungi decompose organic material, they release essential nutrients like nitrogen, phosphorus, and potassium back into the environment. These nutrients then become available to plants, fueling their growth and supporting the entire food web. This intricate web of nutrient exchange highlights the interconnectedness of all living organisms. Fungi act as crucial intermediaries, connecting the living and the dead, ensuring the continuous flow of nutrients within the ecosystem.

The role of fungi in nutrient cycling extends beyond terrestrial ecosystems. In aquatic environments, fungi play a similar role, decomposing organic matter and releasing nutrients back into the water column. This process is particularly important in nutrient-rich environments like wetlands and estuaries, where fungal decomposition helps to maintain water quality and support the diverse communities of aquatic life. Even in the deep ocean, fungal communities contribute to the breakdown of organic matter, playing a vital role in the global carbon cycle.

Specific examples further illuminate the profound influence of fungi on decay and renewal. Consider the white-rot fungi, a group known for their ability to degrade lignin, a complex polymer found in wood. This ability is essential for breaking down woody debris in forests, returning valuable nutrients to the ecosystem. Another example is the mycorrhizal fungi, which form symbiotic relationships with plant roots. These fungi not only enhance nutrient uptake by plants but also protect them from pathogens and improve their tolerance to environmental stress. These intricate partnerships demonstrate the crucial role of fungi in supporting plant health and overall ecosystem resilience.

The study of fungal decay and renewal is a continuous journey of discovery. Scientists are constantly uncovering new species of fungi and learning more about their complex ecological roles. Advanced molecular techniques allow researchers to analyze fungal communities in unprecedented detail, revealing the hidden diversity of these remarkable organisms. This ongoing research is crucial for understanding the intricate workings of ecosystems and developing strategies for conservation and sustainable management of natural resources.

This constant cycle of decay and renewal, driven by the unseen hand of fungal communities, is a testament to the interconnectedness and resilience of life on Earth. It is a reminder that death and decay are not endings, but rather essential stages in the continuous cycle of transformation and rebirth. By understanding the intricate roles of fungi in this cycle, we gain a deeper appreciation for the complex web of life that sustains our planet. And within this web, fungi hold a position of extraordinary importance, orchestrating the symphony of decay and renewal that allows life to flourish.

3.5   Mycorrhizal Magic

The world beneath our feet is a realm of intricate connections, a hidden symphony orchestrated by the delicate threads of mycelia. Among the most fascinating of these fungal interactions are the mycorrhizal networks, symbiotic partnerships between fungi and plant roots. These relationships, often invisible to the naked eye, are fundamental to the health and resilience of terrestrial ecosystems. Mycorrhizal fungi extend the reach of plant roots, acting as microscopic foraging networks that unlock nutrients otherwise unavailable to their plant partners.

Imagine a vast underground web, connecting the roots of trees and other plants in a complex exchange of resources. This is the essence of mycorrhizae. The fungal hyphae, thread-like filaments, weave through the soil, exploring crevices and binding soil particles together. They penetrate the root cells of plants, forming intimate connections where nutrients are traded. Plants provide the fungi with sugars produced through photosynthesis, while the fungi, in return, supply the plants with essential minerals like phosphorus, nitrogen, and micronutrients. This mutually beneficial relationship enhances the plant's ability to absorb water and resist drought, disease, and even toxic heavy metals.

There are two primary types of mycorrhizae: arbuscular mycorrhizae and ectomycorrhizae. Arbuscular mycorrhizae, the more common type, penetrate the cell walls of plant roots, forming tree-like structures called arbuscules within the root cells. These arbuscules are the primary sites of nutrient exchange. Ectomycorrhizae, on the other hand, form a sheath around the root tips and grow between root cells, but do not penetrate the cell walls. They are often associated with trees in temperate and boreal forests, creating a dense network of hyphae that extends outward into the soil. Understanding these distinct types of mycorrhizae and their respective roles in different plant communities provides valuable insight into ecosystem dynamics.

The diversity of mycorrhizal fungi is astonishing. Different fungal species have evolved to partner with specific plant hosts, creating intricate webs of interdependence. A single tree, for instance, can be colonized by dozens of different mycorrhizal fungi, each contributing to the tree's overall health and resilience. This diversity ensures that nutrients are efficiently cycled through the ecosystem, supporting the growth and survival of a wide range of plant species. As a field geologist, I have witnessed firsthand the remarkable ability of mycorrhizae to thrive in a variety of environments, from harsh deserts to lush rainforests.

Exploring the intricate architecture of mycorrhizae requires careful excavation and meticulous observation. Using a trowel and a gentle hand, I carefully expose the root systems of plants, searching for the delicate threads of fungal hyphae. A magnifying glass reveals the intricate structures of these fungal networks, highlighting the intimate connections between fungi and plant roots. Collecting soil samples and examining them under a microscope allows for a deeper understanding of the diversity and abundance of mycorrhizal fungi present in a particular location. These observations, coupled with detailed field notes and photographs, contribute to a comprehensive understanding of the mycorrhizal relationships within a given ecosystem.

The study of mycorrhizae reveals the interconnectedness of life beneath our feet. These symbiotic partnerships play a crucial role in nutrient cycling, plant growth, and ecosystem stability. They enhance the ability of plants to withstand environmental stresses, promoting biodiversity and ecosystem resilience. Understanding the complex interactions within mycorrhizal networks is essential for effective conservation and restoration efforts. By protecting and promoting these vital fungal communities, we can safeguard the health and productivity of our planet's ecosystems.

Mycorrhizal networks also play a critical role in carbon sequestration, storing vast amounts of carbon in the soil. The fungi contribute to soil structure, binding soil particles together and creating stable aggregates that enhance water infiltration and reduce erosion. This improved soil structure facilitates the accumulation of organic matter, locking away carbon and mitigating the effects of climate change. The role of mycorrhizae in carbon sequestration highlights the interconnectedness of the global carbon cycle and the importance of preserving these fungal communities.

Furthermore, research has shown that mycorrhizal networks can facilitate communication between plants. Through the intricate web of hyphae, plants can exchange chemical signals, warning each other of impending threats like insect attacks or drought conditions. This underground communication system allows plants to respond collectively to environmental challenges, enhancing their overall survival. The ability of mycorrhizae to mediate plant communication adds another layer of complexity to the intricate interplay between plants and fungi in the soil.

In conclusion, the "mycorrhizal magic" operating beneath the surface of the earth is a testament to the intricate web of life that sustains our planet. These symbiotic partnerships between fungi and plant roots are not only fundamental to the health and resilience of individual plants but also play a crucial role in shaping entire ecosystems. As we continue to explore the hidden world of mycelia, we uncover new insights into the interconnectedness of life and the vital role that fungi play in maintaining the delicate balance of nature. Understanding and protecting these intricate relationships is essential for ensuring the long-term health and productivity of our planet. The ongoing research into mycorrhizae holds immense promise for sustainable agriculture, forestry, and ecological restoration, paving the way for a future where we work in harmony with nature's intricate systems.

4   Chapter 4: Mapping the Mycelium

Understanding the vast, hidden networks of mycelium requires a unique blend of scientific curiosity and meticulous fieldwork. My approach to mapping these intricate structures has evolved over years of hands-on exploration, incorporating both traditional geological techniques and specialized methods adapted for the delicate nature of fungal growth. Imagine the challenge of tracing a single thread within a massive, interwoven tapestry – that's essentially what we're doing when we try to map the mycelium. This process demands patience, precision, and a deep understanding of the environment in which these organisms thrive.

The initial stages involve careful site selection. I gravitate towards areas with visible fungal fruiting bodies, as these offer clues to the underlying mycelial network. Geological surveys, including soil analysis and assessments of rock formations, help paint a broader picture of the subterranean landscape. Understanding the soil composition, its pH, moisture content, and the presence of specific minerals, is critical. These factors significantly influence the distribution and growth patterns of different fungal species. I often consult geological maps and historical records of the area, looking for patterns that might correlate with fungal presence. This groundwork provides a foundation for more targeted exploration.

Once a promising site is identified, the real work begins. I employ a combination of excavation and non-invasive techniques to uncover the hidden mycelial network. Small, carefully placed trenches allow me to observe the mycelium in its natural environment, noting its depth, density, and connections with surrounding vegetation. I use a variety of tools, including trowels, brushes, and even dental picks, to gently expose the delicate threads without causing damage. For non-invasive mapping, ground-penetrating radar (GPR) can be employed. This technology allows us to visualize the subsurface without disturbing the soil, providing valuable information about the extent and density of the mycelium.

As the mycelium is revealed, meticulous documentation becomes essential. Detailed sketches and photographs are taken, capturing the intricate branching patterns and connections to plant roots. GPS coordinates are recorded to precisely map the location of each sample. Samples of the mycelium are collected and carefully labeled for later laboratory analysis. These samples are crucial for identifying the species present and understanding their genetic diversity. DNA sequencing and microscopic examination provide further insights into the complex interactions within the fungal community.

Interpreting the collected data is like piecing together a complex puzzle. The distribution patterns of different fungal species can reveal important ecological relationships. For instance, the presence of certain mycorrhizal fungi can indicate the types of trees they are associated with. The density and extent of the mycelium can provide clues to the health and productivity of the ecosystem. By analyzing these patterns, we can gain a deeper understanding of the vital role fungi play in nutrient cycling, soil stabilization, and plant growth.

This process of mapping the mycelium is not simply about creating a visual representation of fungal networks. It's about deciphering the language of fungi, understanding their intricate relationships with the environment, and uncovering their hidden influence on the world around us. Each carefully excavated trench, each meticulously documented sample, brings us closer to unraveling the mysteries of this fascinating kingdom. The data we gather contributes to a growing body of knowledge that has far-reaching implications for conservation efforts, agricultural practices, and even medical research. Through careful observation and analysis, we are slowly beginning to appreciate the true extent of the mycelial melody and its profound impact on the Earth's symphony.

4.1 Tools of the Trade

Venturing into the field to study mycelial networks requires a unique set of tools, each serving a specific purpose in unveiling the secrets of this hidden world. A geologist's approach to mycology blends traditional geological techniques with specialized equipment adapted for the delicate task of fungal exploration. Preparation for a day in the field begins with assembling the essentials, ensuring that I have everything needed to navigate diverse terrains and document my findings accurately. My fieldwork toolkit always includes a sturdy geological hammer and chisel, indispensable for accessing rock crevices and examining the interface between stone and soil where fungi often thrive. A hand lens, with its magnifying power, allows me to observe the intricate details of fungal structures, from the delicate gills of mushrooms to the thread-like hyphae that form the mycelium itself. These seemingly simple tools are fundamental for close-range examination of fungal morphology and identifying key characteristics that distinguish different species. A GPS device and detailed topographic maps are essential for navigating remote locations and precisely marking the coordinates of fungal discoveries. This precise mapping allows me to track the distribution of different species and correlate their presence with specific geological features.

Beyond these fundamental tools, my kit also contains specialized equipment designed for the delicate task of collecting and preserving fungal samples. Sterile scalpels and forceps are crucial for taking precise samples without contaminating the surrounding environment or damaging the delicate fungal structures. These samples are carefully placed in breathable containers, often lined with moistened filter paper, to prevent desiccation and preserve their integrity for later analysis. A field notebook and waterproof pens are vital for recording detailed observations, sketching fungal formations, and noting the environmental conditions of each sampling site. These field notes serve as the foundation for later research and analysis, capturing the essence of each discovery in its original context.

Photography plays a crucial role in documenting my findings, and I carry both a high-resolution digital camera and a macro lens. The camera captures the larger context of the fungal habitat, showcasing its relationship to the surrounding environment. The macro lens, however, allows me to delve into the microscopic world, revealing the intricate details of fungal structures often invisible to the naked eye. These photographs become an invaluable record, allowing me to revisit and analyze my findings long after leaving the field.

Soil sampling equipment is another critical component of my toolkit. A soil auger and various coring tools enable me to extract samples from different depths, revealing the vertical distribution of mycelial networks within the soil profile. These samples can then be analyzed in the lab to determine soil composition, pH levels, and other factors that influence fungal growth. This information provides valuable insights into the complex interplay between geology, soil properties, and the distribution of fungal communities.

Back in the lab, the collected samples and data are subjected to further scrutiny. A dissecting microscope, equipped with powerful illumination, allows for detailed examination of fungal morphology and identification of key characteristics. Preparing microscope slides requires specialized tools like microtomes for creating thin sections of fungal tissue, stains for highlighting specific structures, and cover slips for protecting the specimens. These prepared slides are then examined under a compound microscope, revealing the intricate cellular structures of the fungi and aiding in precise species identification.

Further analysis often involves culturing fungal samples in the lab. Petri dishes filled with agar media provide a controlled environment for fungal growth, allowing me to observe their development and isolate individual species for study. Incubators maintain optimal temperature and humidity conditions, promoting healthy fungal growth and ensuring reliable results. These culturing techniques are essential for studying the physiology and behavior of fungi under controlled conditions.

Finally, digital resources and specialized software play an increasingly important role in modern mycological research. Online databases and identification keys provide access to a vast repository of fungal knowledge, assisting with species identification and expanding our understanding of fungal diversity. Geographic Information Systems (GIS) software allows me to integrate my field data with spatial information, creating detailed maps that visualize the distribution of fungal communities and their relationship to the surrounding environment. These tools, when combined with meticulous fieldwork, offer a comprehensive approach to unraveling the mysteries of the mycelial world, revealing its hidden connections to the broader ecosystem and furthering our understanding of its crucial role in the Earth's intricate web of life.

4.2   Charting the Unknown

Precisely mapping the sprawling, often invisible, networks of mycelium requires a blend of traditional geological surveying techniques and an understanding of fungal ecology. Consider the mycelium as a subterranean landscape, with its own contours, valleys, and peaks, albeit on a microscopic scale. Our task is to chart this hidden terrain, revealing the intricate connections that weave through the soil.

One primary tool in this endeavor is the use of transects. These carefully measured lines, laid out across a study area, provide a framework for systematic sampling. Along these transects, we dig small pits, carefully documenting the soil profile and the presence of any visible mycelium. This methodical approach allows us to build a picture of the mycelium's distribution, revealing patterns linked to vegetation, moisture levels, and other environmental factors. Imagine these transects as cross-sections through a hidden world, each pit a window into the subterranean activities of fungi.

Beyond simple observation, soil coring techniques provide a deeper glimpse into the mycelial world. These cylindrical samples, extracted from the earth, offer a three-dimensional perspective on the distribution of fungal hyphae. By carefully analyzing the soil cores, we can identify different fungal species based on their unique hyphal characteristics, such as color, branching patterns, and the presence of reproductive structures. Think of each core as a miniature geological record, preserving the history of fungal growth within that specific location.

Sophisticated laboratory analysis adds another layer of precision to our mapping efforts. DNA sequencing, for example, allows us to identify fungi even in the absence of visible fruiting bodies. This technique is especially valuable for understanding the diversity of mycorrhizal fungi, which often lack conspicuous above-ground structures. We can extract fungal DNA directly from soil samples and compare it to existing databases, effectively creating a genetic fingerprint of the fungal community. This intricate process resembles detective work, piecing together the identity of unseen organisms through their genetic code.

Geophysical methods, traditionally used to study larger-scale geological features, can also be adapted to map mycelium. Ground-penetrating radar (GPR), for example, can detect changes in soil density and moisture content, indirectly revealing the presence of extensive mycelial networks. While this technique doesn't provide species-specific information, it offers a broader perspective on the distribution of mycelium across the landscape. Imagine using GPR as a sonar system, bouncing signals off the hidden contours of the mycelial world to create a subterranean map. Furthermore, isotopic analysis can be employed to trace the flow of nutrients through mycelial networks. By analyzing the isotopic signatures of carbon and nitrogen within fungal tissues and surrounding plant roots, we can map the intricate pathways of nutrient exchange facilitated by mycorrhizal fungi. This technique allows us to visualize the hidden connections between plants and fungi, revealing the complex web of symbiotic relationships that underpin ecosystem health. Picture isotopic analysis as tracing the flow of colored dyes through a hidden network of pipes, illuminating the connections between different components of the system.

Documenting our findings accurately and effectively is crucial. Detailed field notes, precise GPS coordinates, and carefully labeled samples form the foundation of our mycelial maps. We combine these traditional methods with digital mapping software, creating georeferenced databases that allow us to visualize and analyze our data in new ways. Imagine these digital maps as dynamic portraits of the mycelial landscape, constantly evolving as we gather more information.

Mapping mycelium is not simply a technical exercise; it is an act of discovery. It reveals the intricate connections that bind together the subterranean world and provides valuable insights into the vital role fungi play in maintaining ecosystem health. As we chart the unknown, we unveil a hidden world of remarkable complexity and beauty, a world that holds immense potential for understanding the interconnectedness of life on Earth. These insights, gleaned from the meticulous work of mapping, remind us that beneath our feet lies a hidden kingdom, intricately woven into the fabric of our planet. The careful mapping of mycelium is therefore not just a scientific endeavor, but a journey of exploration, revealing the hidden architecture of nature's most vital networks. As we develop more advanced techniques and tools, we will undoubtedly unveil further secrets of these extraordinary organisms and their crucial role in our planet's ecosystems.

4.3 The Language of Fungi

Fungi don't speak in human tongues, yet they communicate in a language far older and more subtle than our own. This language isn't spoken with vocal cords, but expressed through intricate chemical signals, electrical impulses, and the very architecture of the mycelial network itself. Decoding these messages is key to understanding the hidden world beneath our feet, a world that plays a vital role in the health and function of our planet's ecosystems. One aspect of this fungal communication involves the release and reception of chemical compounds. These compounds act as messengers, transmitting information about nutrient availability, potential threats, and even the presence of compatible mating partners. Think of it as an intricate olfactory system, a vast network of scent trails invisible to the human eye, yet constantly shaping the interactions within the soil.

The intricate network of hyphae, the thread-like filaments that make up the mycelium, forms a complex communication highway. Electrical signals, remarkably similar to those in our own nervous systems, travel through these hyphal pathways. These signals can transmit information rapidly across vast distances within the mycelial network, coordinating growth, resource allocation, and responses to environmental changes. Imagine a forest floor pulsating with these silent electrical conversations, a hidden network buzzing with activity.

The architecture of the mycelium itself holds clues to its communication strategies. The branching patterns of hyphae, the density of the network, and the formation of specialized structures like rhizomorphs (thick, root-like strands of mycelium) all contribute to the efficient flow of information and resources. These structures facilitate the transport of nutrients and water over long distances, enabling fungi to thrive in diverse environments and respond effectively to changing conditions. Picture the mycelium as a living, breathing map, constantly adapting and evolving in response to the messages flowing through its intricate network.

Geologists, with their understanding of earth processes and spatial relationships, are uniquely positioned to decipher this intricate fungal language. By studying the distribution of fungal communities across different landscapes, we can begin to understand the environmental factors that influence their communication patterns. Soil composition, moisture levels, temperature gradients, and the presence of other organisms all play a role in shaping the mycelial network and its communication dynamics. A field geologist's trained eye can discern subtle shifts in these factors, revealing hidden connections between the fungal world and the larger ecosystem.

Mapping the mycelium requires a combination of traditional fieldwork and cutting-edge technology. Careful observation and meticulous documentation of fungal fruiting bodies provide valuable insights into the distribution and diversity of fungal species. Soil sampling and analysis reveal the chemical signatures of fungal activity, offering clues about their communication strategies. Sophisticated imaging techniques, such as scanning electron microscopy, allow us to peer into the microscopic world of hyphae, revealing the intricate architecture of the mycelial network. Combining these approaches provides a multi-faceted perspective on the fungal language, allowing us to decode its complexities.

Consider the example of mycorrhizal networks, the symbiotic partnerships between fungi and plant roots. These networks facilitate communication not only between the fungus and its plant partner, but also between different plants within the same ecosystem. Through the mycelial network, plants can exchange nutrients, warn each other of impending threats, and even support the growth of seedlings. This underground communication network, mediated by fungi, plays a vital role in the stability and resilience of plant communities. Understanding the intricacies of these interactions requires careful observation and analysis of the mycelial network, uncovering the hidden messages that shape the lives of both fungi and plants.

The study of fungal communication is a relatively young field, and there is much we still don't understand. However, the more we learn about the language of fungi, the more we appreciate their crucial role in the health of our planet. By deciphering their intricate communication systems, we can gain insights into the complex web of life that connects all living things. This knowledge can inform conservation efforts, help us develop sustainable agricultural practices, and even inspire new medical treatments. The fungal world, once hidden beneath our feet, is now revealing its secrets, offering a glimpse into a language far older and more complex than our own. As we continue to explore this hidden realm, we unlock a deeper understanding of the interconnectedness of life on Earth and the vital role fungi play in maintaining its delicate balance. This pursuit requires patience, curiosity, and a willingness to listen to the whispers of the earth, deciphering the subtle language of the mycelial network that connects us all.

5 Chapter 5: A Geologist's Journey

My fascination with the natural world began not in the depths of a forest or the heart of a mountain range, but in the seemingly mundane cracks of my childhood sidewalk. Tiny, resilient weeds pushing through concrete, the intricate patterns of lichen on rocks, and the occasional mushroom bravely emerging after a rain shower sparked an early curiosity about the unseen forces shaping our environment. This fascination, initially diffuse, gradually crystallized into a focused interest in geology, the study of Earth's physical structure and substance. I envisioned myself deciphering the stories etched in stone, unraveling the mysteries held within ancient landscapes. This nascent passion led me to pursue a degree in geology, opening doors to a world I could only have dreamed of.

University life was a whirlwind of lectures, lab work, and field trips, each experience deepening my understanding of Earth's intricate tapestry. I was particularly captivated by the interplay between geological processes and biological life, especially in extreme environments. My professors, recognizing this burgeoning interest, encouraged me to explore the field of geobiology, a discipline that investigates the co-evolution of Earth and its inhabitants. One pivotal moment came during a field expedition to the Canadian Shield, a vast expanse of ancient rock. While my classmates focused on mapping the exposed formations, I found myself drawn to the thin layer of soil and the surprisingly vibrant microbial communities thriving within it. This seemingly insignificant layer represented a crucial interface between the geological and biological realms, a realization that would shape the trajectory of my career.

I shifted my focus to the microscopic world, specifically the intricate networks of fungi that permeate the Earth's subsurface. These often-overlooked organisms play a critical role in nutrient cycling, rock weathering, and soil formation. My geological training provided a unique perspective, allowing me to examine the influence of geological substrates on fungal diversity and distribution. Early fieldwork adventures took me to diverse landscapes, from the arid deserts of the American Southwest to the lush rainforests of the Amazon Basin. Each environment presented unique challenges and rewards, offering glimpses into the remarkable adaptability and resilience of fungal life. I recall one particularly memorable expedition to Iceland, a land of fire and ice. There, amidst the stark volcanic landscapes, I discovered thriving communities of fungi adapted to extreme temperatures and nutrient-poor conditions.

These early experiences solidified my passion for studying the hidden world of fungi. The more I learned, the more I realized how little we truly understood about these remarkable organisms. My research gradually evolved to focus on the role of fungi in shaping Earth's surface. I investigated how fungal hyphae, the thread-like filaments that make up the mycelium, interact with minerals, influencing weathering processes and soil development. This interdisciplinary approach, combining geological and biological principles, allowed me to explore questions that had previously been overlooked. I found myself pushing the boundaries of traditional geological research, embracing the challenges and complexities of this emerging field. One particularly rewarding aspect of my journey has been the opportunity to collaborate with researchers from diverse disciplines. Working with soil scientists, microbiologists, and ecologists has broadened my perspective and enriched my understanding of the interconnectedness of life. These collaborations have led to exciting discoveries, revealing the intricate ways in which fungi influence everything from plant growth to carbon cycling. Looking back, my path from sidewalk cracks to scientific exploration has been a winding one, filled with unexpected turns and discoveries. It has been a journey driven by curiosity, fueled by passion, and shaped by the remarkable world of fungi.

5.1 Early Inspirations

My fascination with the natural world began not in the hushed halls of academia, but in the vibrant chaos of my grandmother's garden. She wasn't a scientist, not in the traditional sense, but she possessed a deep, intuitive understanding of the earth's rhythms. I spent countless childhood hours trailing behind her as she tended her rows of tomatoes and beans, her hands stained with soil, her face alight with quiet joy. It wasn't the brightly colored blooms that captivated me, though, but the rich, dark earth beneath our feet. I remember digging my fingers into the cool soil, marveling at the intricate network of roots and the strange, white threads that wove between them. My grandmother, noticing my curiosity, explained that these were the "hidden helpers" of the garden, the mycelium that nourished the plants. This early exposure ignited within me a spark, a profound curiosity about the unseen forces shaping the world around us. It was a fascination that would eventually lead me to the study of geology and, later, to a lifelong pursuit of understanding the intricate melodies of the mycelial world.

This nascent interest in the subterranean world was further fueled by a tattered copy of "The Field Guide to Mushrooms" I discovered tucked away in the attic. The book, with its detailed illustrations and descriptions of fantastical fungal forms, opened my eyes to a realm of biodiversity I had never imagined. I pored over its pages, captivated by the sheer variety of shapes, sizes, and colors, from the delicate parasol mushrooms to the shelf-like bracket fungi clinging to decaying logs. Each species seemed to possess its own unique personality, its own story to tell. I began to see the world differently, no longer just a collection of plants and animals, but a complex tapestry woven together by the unseen threads of the fungal kingdom. This newfound perspective transformed my childhood explorations, every walk in the woods becoming a treasure hunt for hidden fungal wonders. I was no longer simply walking through nature, I was walking within it, acutely aware of the vibrant life teeming beneath the surface.

These early experiences laid the foundation for my future academic pursuits. While my initial focus in college was geology, the allure of the fungal world never truly left me. I found myself drawn to courses that explored the interplay between the lithosphere and the biosphere, the ways in which geological processes shaped the environment and influenced the distribution of life. One particular professor, Dr. Eleanor Vance, a renowned soil ecologist, recognized my passion and encouraged me to pursue research on the relationship between soil composition and fungal diversity. Under her mentorship, I began to delve into the scientific literature, learning about the crucial role fungi play in nutrient cycling, soil formation, and ecosystem health. Her guidance was invaluable, providing me with the tools and knowledge to explore the intricate connections between the geological and fungal realms. The summer after my junior year, I had the opportunity to join Dr. Vance on a research expedition to the old-growth forests of the Pacific Northwest. It was my first real fieldwork experience, and it proved to be a transformative journey. Surrounded by towering trees and the damp, earthy scent of the forest floor, I felt a profound sense of connection to the natural world. We spent our days collecting soil samples, identifying fungal species, and mapping the distribution of mycelial networks. The work was challenging, often requiring us to hike for miles through dense undergrowth, but it was also incredibly rewarding. Every new discovery, every glimpse into the hidden world beneath our feet, fueled my passion for research. It was during this expedition that I witnessed firsthand the sheer power and resilience of fungal life. We came across a massive, fallen log, seemingly lifeless and decaying. But upon closer inspection, we discovered that it was teeming with fungal activity. A vibrant tapestry of mycelium had colonized the log, breaking down the wood and releasing nutrients back into the soil. This process of decay, often seen as an ending, was in fact a beginning, a vital step in the cycle of life. It was a profound realization, one that cemented my fascination with the fungal kingdom and its essential role in the interconnectedness of all living things. This experience, more than any textbook or lecture, solidified my commitment to unraveling the mysteries of the mycelial world. It was the culmination of years of quiet observation and growing curiosity, a testament to the power of early influences and the enduring allure of the natural world. From the humble beginnings in my grandmother's garden to the depths of the ancient forests, my journey had just begun.

5.2 Fieldwork Adventures

The biting wind whipped across the Icelandic highlands, a constant companion to the rhythmic crunch of my boots on the volcanic scree. This desolate landscape, seemingly barren at first glance, held a hidden world beneath its surface, a world I was eager to explore. My geological hammer, usually employed for chipping away at ancient rock formations, now served a different purpose – gently uncovering the delicate threads of mycelia weaving through the thin layer of soil clinging to the volcanic slopes. I recall the initial shock, not at finding the fungi, but at its sheer tenacity in such a harsh environment. Life, it seemed, found a way even in the most improbable of places.

That expedition to Iceland, early in my career, remains etched in my memory. It solidified my understanding that the study of geology and mycology are intrinsically linked. The composition of the volcanic rock, its porous nature allowing for water retention, and the slow, steady weathering process – all these factors contributed to creating a unique microhabitat for these hardy fungal species. I learned to recognize the subtle signs – the almost imperceptible lift of the soil, the faint earthy aroma clinging to the air – that hinted at the presence of mycelial networks beneath my feet. Each discovery felt like unearthing a secret, a whispered conversation between the earth and its hidden inhabitants.

The following year, I found myself in the humid rainforests of the Amazon basin, a world away from the stark beauty of Iceland. Here, the abundance of life was overwhelming. Every surface, from the towering trees to the fallen logs decaying on the forest floor, pulsed with fungal activity. The air hung thick with the scent of damp earth and the sweet, musky aroma of countless fungal species. My fieldwork here involved meticulous mapping of the vast mycelial networks that interconnected the entire forest ecosystem. I spent hours crawling through the undergrowth, tracing the delicate threads of mycelium as they wound their way through the leaf litter, binding the forest together in a complex web of life.

This experience highlighted the stark contrast between fungal ecosystems in different environments. While the Icelandic fungi clung precariously to life in a harsh landscape, the Amazonian fungi thrived in a riot of biodiversity. Yet, despite their differences, both played a crucial role in their respective ecosystems. This realization deepened my fascination with the adaptability and resilience of fungi, their ability to thrive in environments as diverse as volcanic slopes and tropical rainforests.

Later, in the dry, cracked earth of the Atacama Desert in Chile, I encountered another extreme. This seemingly lifeless landscape held another surprise. Beneath the parched surface, specialized fungi formed symbiotic relationships with the sparse vegetation, enabling these plants to survive in the arid conditions. These hardy organisms were masters of water conservation, their mycelial networks extending deep into the soil to access hidden moisture. Studying these fungi required a different approach, involving careful excavation and microscopic analysis to understand their intricate adaptations to this extreme environment. The meticulous work, however, yielded invaluable insights into the resilience of life and the critical role fungi play in even the most challenging ecosystems.

One particularly memorable expedition took me to the ancient forests of the Pacific Northwest. Here, amidst towering redwood trees, I encountered some of the largest and oldest organisms on Earth – massive mycelial networks that spanned hectares of forest floor. These ancient networks, some estimated to be thousands of years old, played a vital role in maintaining the health and stability of the forest ecosystem. Walking among these giants, I felt a profound sense of awe and respect for the intricate interconnectedness of life. The quiet hum of the forest, the rustling of leaves overhead, the scent of damp earth and decaying wood – all spoke to the vital role of these hidden fungal networks.

Each fieldwork experience has been a lesson in adaptation, resilience, and interconnectedness. From the frozen landscapes of Iceland to the lush rainforests of the Amazon, the dry deserts of Chile, and the ancient forests of the Pacific Northwest, I've witnessed the remarkable diversity and vital role of fungi in shaping our planet. These adventures have not only deepened my scientific understanding but also fostered a deep appreciation for the intricate beauty and hidden wonders of the natural world. The wind, the rain, the scorching sun, the biting cold – these elements became my constant companions, shaping my understanding of the earth and the remarkable organisms that call it home. The journey continues, and with every expedition, I anticipate uncovering more secrets of the mycelial world, each discovery a testament to the enduring power of life on Earth. The melody of mycelia, it seems, is a global symphony, played out in countless variations across the diverse landscapes of our planet.

6 Chapter 6: Mycelia and Mankind

The intertwined history of humanity and fungi is a complex tapestry woven with threads of both benefit and adversity. From the earliest days, fungi have played a pivotal role, sometimes subtly, sometimes dramatically, in shaping human existence. Consider the sobering impact of fungal pathogens on agriculture, capable of decimating crops and leading to widespread famine, like the devastating potato blight of the 19th century that reshaped the demographic landscape of Ireland. Conversely, the fermentation processes driven by microscopic fungi have gifted us with bread, cheese, and alcoholic beverages, cornerstones of culinary tradition and social gathering across cultures. This delicate balance between friend and foe defines our ongoing relationship with the fungal kingdom.

Our ancestors, lacking the sophisticated tools of modern science, often viewed fungi with a mixture of awe and suspicion. Mushrooms, the fruiting bodies of certain fungi, emerged mysteriously from the earth, their sudden appearance after rainfall adding to their mystique. Some were recognized for their nutritional value, while others, possessing potent toxins, were rightfully feared. This inherent duality likely fueled the folklore and mythology surrounding fungi in many cultures, from tales of fairy rings and enchanted forests to warnings of poisonous toadstools. The ethnomycological knowledge accumulated over generations, passed down through oral traditions, often held the key to distinguishing between sustenance and danger within the fungal realm.

The burgeoning field of medicinal mycology represents a frontier of scientific discovery, revealing the remarkable potential of fungi to combat disease. Penicillin, derived from the Penicillium mold, revolutionized medicine in the 20th century, ushering in the era of antibiotics. Today, researchers are exploring the therapeutic properties of a wide range of fungal compounds, seeking new treatments for cancer, viral infections, and neurological disorders. Compounds like psilocybin, found in certain mushrooms, are being investigated for their potential to alleviate depression and anxiety, opening up exciting new avenues for mental health treatment.

Moving beyond medicine, the unique properties of mycelia are inspiring innovation in diverse fields. Mycelial materials, grown from fungal biomass, are being developed as sustainable alternatives to plastics and leather. Their inherent strength, flexibility, and biodegradability make them promising candidates for packaging, construction materials, and even textiles. Furthermore, the ability of mycelia to decompose organic waste offers potential solutions for bioremediation, cleaning up polluted environments and promoting sustainable waste management practices. The intricate network structure of mycelia is also being explored in computing and robotics, inspiring the design of decentralized and adaptive systems.

The preservation of fungal biodiversity is crucial, not only for the health of ecosystems but also for the future of human well-being. Fungi play indispensable roles in nutrient cycling, soil formation, and the intricate web of life that supports all terrestrial ecosystems. However, habitat loss, pollution, and climate change pose significant threats to fungal populations worldwide. Conservation efforts, including the establishment of protected areas, sustainable forestry practices, and citizen science initiatives focused on fungal monitoring, are essential to safeguarding this vital component of biodiversity. Educating the public about the importance of fungi and their ecological roles is paramount for fostering a sense of stewardship and ensuring the long-term survival of these remarkable organisms.

The culinary uses of fungi extend far beyond the familiar button mushrooms found in grocery stores. Across the globe, diverse cultures have incorporated a wide array of edible fungi into their culinary traditions. From the prized truffles of Europe to the shiitake and oyster mushrooms cultivated in Asia, these culinary treasures offer unique flavors, textures, and nutritional benefits. The foraging and cultivation of edible mushrooms provide livelihoods for communities worldwide and contribute to the rich tapestry of global gastronomy. As our understanding of fungal diversity grows, so too does our appreciation for the culinary possibilities offered by this extraordinary kingdom.

Looking towards the future, the potential of mycelia seems boundless. Researchers are exploring the use of fungi in biomining, extracting valuable metals from ores in a more environmentally friendly manner than traditional mining practices. The ability of fungi to break down complex organic molecules holds promise for developing new biofuels and bioplastics, reducing our reliance on fossil fuels. As we delve deeper into the hidden world of fungi, we are continually uncovering new wonders and potential applications that could revolutionize various aspects of human society. This ongoing exploration underscores the importance of continued research and the need to protect the remarkable biodiversity of the fungal kingdom. The symphony of mycelia, once a whisper beneath our feet, is now emerging as a powerful force for innovation and sustainability, shaping a future where nature and technology harmonize to create a more resilient and vibrant world.

6.1   Fungal Friends and Foes

The intimate relationship between humans and fungi stretches back millennia, a complex interplay of dependence and destruction. Consider the humble yeast, a single-celled fungus responsible for the leavening of bread and the fermentation of wine and beer. These culinary cornerstones of many cultures wouldn't exist without the transformative power of this microscopic organism. For thousands of years, we have unknowingly cultivated and utilized yeasts, shaping our diets and social rituals around their activity. This ancient partnership showcases the profound influence fungi have exerted on human civilization. Yet, for every beneficial interaction, there exists a darker side, a reminder of the delicate balance we maintain with this kingdom.

Take, for example, the devastating impact of fungal pathogens on agriculture. Blights, rusts, and smuts, carried by wind and water, can decimate entire crops, threatening food security and economic stability. The Irish Potato Famine of the 19th century, caused by the water mold Phytophthora infestans, serves as a stark reminder of the catastrophic consequences of fungal disease. Millions starved, and countless others were forced to emigrate, altering the course of history. This historical tragedy underscores the vulnerability of human populations to the destructive power of pathogenic fungi. Even today, fungal infections in crops pose a significant challenge to global food production, requiring constant vigilance and innovative solutions.

Moving beyond the realm of agriculture, fungi also present direct threats to human health. Mycoses, infections caused by fungi, range from superficial skin irritations like athlete's foot to life-threatening systemic diseases that attack vital organs. Individuals with compromised immune systems are particularly vulnerable, highlighting the crucial role of a healthy immune response in defending against fungal invaders. Aspergillus, a common mold found in the environment, can cause severe respiratory illness in susceptible individuals, illustrating the potential dangers lurking even in seemingly innocuous fungi. The development of antifungal medications has been a crucial advancement in managing these infections, though resistance to these treatments remains an ongoing concern, driving the need for continued research and development of new therapeutic strategies.

Conversely, fungi also offer immense potential in medicine. Penicillin, derived from the Penicillium mold, revolutionized healthcare in the 20th century, ushering in the era of antibiotics. This groundbreaking discovery dramatically reduced mortality rates from bacterial infections and paved the way for the development of numerous other life-saving drugs. Beyond antibiotics, fungi are also sources of valuable compounds with immunosuppressant and cholesterol-lowering properties, demonstrating their diverse pharmacological applications. Cyclosporine, derived from a soil fungus, is essential in organ transplantation, preventing rejection and enabling countless lives to be saved. Ongoing research continues to explore the vast potential of fungi as a source of novel pharmaceuticals, offering hope for treating a wide array of diseases.

Beyond their direct impact on human health and agriculture, fungi play a crucial ecological role as decomposers. They break down organic matter, releasing essential nutrients back into the ecosystem. This process of decay and renewal is fundamental to the cycling of nutrients, driving the vitality and productivity of ecosystems worldwide. Without the tireless work of these fungal recyclers, the world would be overwhelmed by accumulating dead plant and animal material, disrupting the delicate balance of life. From the forest floor to the deepest ocean trenches, fungi are essential players in the intricate web of life, ensuring the continuous flow of energy and nutrients. Their role in decomposition is particularly vital in maintaining the health of forests, breaking down fallen leaves and wood, and enriching the soil. This process also contributes to carbon sequestration, playing a crucial role in regulating the global carbon cycle and mitigating climate change.

Moreover, certain fungi form symbiotic relationships with plant roots, creating mycorrhizal networks that enhance nutrient uptake. These mutually beneficial partnerships enable plants to access essential nutrients like phosphorus and nitrogen more efficiently, promoting their growth and resilience. This intricate underground network of fungal hyphae extends the reach of plant roots, creating a vast interconnected system that facilitates communication and resource sharing among plants. Mycorrhizal fungi play a vital role in maintaining the health and stability of plant communities, particularly in nutrient-poor environments. The discovery and understanding of these complex symbiotic relationships has revolutionized our understanding of plant ecology and underscored the importance of preserving fungal biodiversity.

As we delve deeper into the intricacies of the fungal kingdom, we uncover a vast and largely unexplored frontier. The potential of fungi to address pressing global challenges, from developing sustainable agriculture to combating climate change, remains largely untapped. Further research into the diverse functions of fungi and their intricate interactions with other organisms is essential for harnessing their full potential. This exploration requires a multidisciplinary approach, bringing together mycologists, geologists, ecologists, and other scientists to unravel the complex mysteries of the fungal world. As we continue to learn about the remarkable capabilities of fungi, we can better appreciate their vital role in shaping our planet and its future. The ongoing quest to understand the melody of mycelia is a testament to the enduring power of scientific curiosity and the profound impact of these often-overlooked organisms on the interconnectedness of life.

6.2   The Future of Fungi

The convergence of scientific advancement and ecological awareness paints a vibrant, albeit complex, picture of the future roles fungi will play in our world. Consider the burgeoning field of mycoremediation, where fungi are employed as nature's tiny cleanup crews, diligently detoxifying polluted environments. Specific fungal species demonstrate a remarkable ability to break down harmful pollutants, from heavy metals to pesticides and even plastics, offering sustainable solutions for environmental restoration. This potential extends to addressing industrial waste, transforming hazardous byproducts into less toxic substances. Imagine landscapes revitalized, not by expensive human intervention, but through the quiet, efficient work of fungal networks. This ability to decompose complex organic compounds extends beyond pollution remediation, playing a critical role in nutrient cycling within ecosystems, ensuring the continued health and productivity of our planet's natural landscapes.

Furthermore, the unique architecture of fungal mycelia provides a fascinating template for new materials. Researchers are exploring the use of mycelium as a sustainable building material, creating biodegradable bricks and insulation. Its intricate network of hyphae creates a strong, lightweight material with impressive thermal and acoustic properties. Picture a future where homes and buildings are grown, not built, minimizing environmental impact and utilizing a readily renewable resource. This approach aligns perfectly with principles of circular economy and sustainable design, offering promising alternatives to traditional construction materials. Beyond construction, mycelium also holds potential in packaging, textiles, and even furniture, replacing synthetic materials with a biodegradable, eco-friendly option. The medical applications of fungi are also expanding rapidly. Beyond the well-established use of penicillin and other antibiotics derived from fungi, researchers are investigating the potential of various species for treating a range of ailments, including cancer, viral infections, and neurological disorders. Specific compounds found in certain mushrooms exhibit powerful immunomodulatory and anti-inflammatory effects, opening new avenues for drug development. This research delves into the intricate biochemical pathways within fungi, seeking to unlock the therapeutic potential hidden within these remarkable organisms. Traditional medicine practices have long utilized the healing properties of fungi, and modern science is now catching up, validating and expanding on this ancient wisdom.

Agricultural practices are also being revolutionized by our deepening understanding of fungal networks. Mycorrhizal fungi, which form symbiotic relationships with plant roots, are essential for enhancing nutrient uptake and improving plant health. By fostering these beneficial fungal partnerships, farmers can reduce their reliance on chemical fertilizers and pesticides, promoting sustainable agriculture. Specific fungal species can also protect plants from pathogens, acting as a natural defense system against diseases. This translates into increased crop yields, enhanced resilience to environmental stresses, and a reduction in the ecological footprint of agriculture. The intricate interplay between fungi, plants, and the surrounding soil environment offers a complex and dynamic system for sustainable food production.

While the potential benefits of fungi are vast, there are also crucial conservation concerns to address. Habitat loss due to deforestation, urbanization, and agricultural expansion poses a significant threat to fungal diversity. Climate change further exacerbates these pressures, altering temperature and precipitation patterns, impacting fungal growth and distribution. Protecting existing fungal habitats and promoting responsible land management practices are vital for safeguarding the biodiversity of these critical organisms. The intricate web of life within ecosystems relies heavily on the contributions of fungi, and their loss could have cascading effects on overall ecological health. Efforts to document and understand fungal diversity are also crucial, providing baseline data for monitoring changes and implementing effective conservation strategies.

The exploration of fungal genomes promises to unlock even more secrets hidden within these enigmatic organisms. By unraveling the genetic code of various fungal species, we can gain deeper insights into their evolutionary history, metabolic pathways, and ecological roles. This knowledge will pave the way for targeted applications in biotechnology, medicine, and environmental remediation. The vast genetic diversity within the fungal kingdom holds immense potential for discovering novel enzymes, bioactive compounds, and other valuable resources. Furthermore, understanding the genetic mechanisms underlying fungal adaptations to different environments can help us predict and mitigate the impacts of climate change on these crucial organisms.

The future of fungi is inextricably linked to our own. As we continue to unravel the mysteries of the mycelial world, we uncover a wealth of potential solutions to some of the most pressing challenges facing humanity. From cleaning up polluted environments and developing sustainable materials to revolutionizing medicine and agriculture, fungi offer a path towards a more sustainable and harmonious future. Embracing the potential of these remarkable organisms requires a concerted effort in research, conservation, and education, ensuring that the melody of mycelia continues to enrich our planet for generations to come. This journey of discovery promises not only scientific breakthroughs but also a deeper appreciation for the interconnectedness of life and the vital role that fungi play in the intricate tapestry of our planet's ecosystems.

6.3 Conservation Efforts

The delicate balance of fungal ecosystems is increasingly threatened. Human activities, often driven by short-term gains, disrupt the intricate web of life beneath our feet. Deforestation, a major culprit, strips away the protective canopy and exposes the forest floor to harsh elements. This disrupts the delicate microclimates that many fungal species require, leading to their decline. Intensive agriculture, with its reliance on chemical fertilizers and pesticides, further damages the soil microbiome, harming beneficial fungi and disrupting the natural balance of the ecosystem. Urban sprawl, too, contributes to habitat loss, fragmenting fungal networks and isolating populations. We must recognize that these seemingly disparate actions have far-reaching consequences for the fungal world.

Protecting these vital organisms requires a multi-pronged approach. Establishing protected areas, such as nature reserves and national parks, is crucial for preserving intact fungal habitats. These designated zones provide safe havens for diverse fungal communities, allowing them to thrive undisturbed. However, simply designating an area as protected is not enough. Careful management practices are essential to ensure the long-term health of these ecosystems. This includes controlling invasive species, which can outcompete native fungi, and regulating human activities within the protected zones to minimize disturbance. Moreover, restoring degraded habitats is equally important. Reforestation efforts, for instance, can help rebuild the forest canopy and restore the favorable microclimates that fungi need to flourish. This involves planting native tree species and implementing sustainable forestry practices.

Beyond protected areas, promoting sustainable land management practices is key to safeguarding fungal biodiversity in human-dominated landscapes. In agriculture, reducing reliance on chemical inputs and adopting organic farming methods can create a healthier soil environment for beneficial fungi. No-till farming, which minimizes soil disturbance, can also help preserve fungal networks. In urban areas, incorporating green spaces and utilizing permeable surfaces can provide habitats for fungi and enhance the overall health of the urban ecosystem. Citizen science initiatives, where members of the public participate in data collection and monitoring, offer a valuable tool for tracking fungal populations and assessing the effectiveness of conservation efforts. By engaging local communities in these projects, we can raise awareness about the importance of fungal conservation and empower individuals to take action. Educating landowners and policymakers about the ecological value of fungi is also crucial. By highlighting the essential role that fungi play in nutrient cycling, soil health, and plant growth, we can encourage more informed decisions about land use and management.

Research plays a vital role in guiding conservation efforts. Scientists are constantly working to expand our understanding of fungal diversity, distribution, and ecological roles. By identifying areas of high fungal biodiversity, we can prioritize conservation efforts in these regions. Studying the specific threats faced by different fungal species allows us to develop targeted conservation strategies. For example, understanding the sensitivity of certain fungi to pollution can inform policies aimed at reducing air and water contamination. Investigating the complex interactions between fungi and other organisms helps us appreciate the interconnectedness of ecosystems and the importance of preserving their integrity. Furthermore, exploring the potential of fungi in bioremediation, the use of organisms to clean up pollutants, offers promising avenues for environmental restoration.

Effective conservation requires collaboration. International cooperation is essential for addressing global threats to fungal biodiversity, such as climate change. Sharing knowledge and resources across borders allows countries to learn from each other's experiences and implement more effective conservation strategies. Working together, we can create a global network of protected areas and promote sustainable land management practices on a larger scale. Partnerships between scientists, conservationists, policymakers, and local communities are also vital. By combining scientific expertise with local knowledge and community involvement, we can develop more holistic and effective conservation approaches. The conservation of fungal biodiversity is not merely a scientific endeavor; it is a shared responsibility. We all have a role to play in protecting these remarkable organisms and ensuring the health of our planet. By working together, we can safeguard the future of fungi and the countless ecosystems they support. The intricate melodies of mycelia must continue to resonate through the earth's ecosystems for generations to come.

6.4 Mycelia in Medicine

The earth beneath our feet holds a vast, untapped pharmacopoeia within its fungal networks. For millennia, humans have recognized the healing potential of fungi, from traditional folk remedies to the development of cutting-edge pharmaceuticals. This exploration into the medicinal marvels of mycelia unveils a realm of possibilities, highlighting the ongoing research and remarkable discoveries that are transforming modern medicine. Consider the remarkable story of penicillin, a discovery that revolutionized healthcare. Derived from the Penicillium fungus, this antibiotic has saved countless lives by effectively combating bacterial infections. This single example underscores the immense power of fungal metabolites as sources of life-saving drugs.

Beyond penicillin, a diverse array of fungi contributes to our arsenal of medicines. Cyclosporin, a crucial immunosuppressant derived from the Tolypocladium inflatum fungus, has transformed organ transplantation by reducing the risk of rejection. Statins, cholesterol-lowering drugs sourced from fungi like Aspergillus terreus, are widely prescribed to manage cardiovascular health. These examples represent just the tip of the iceberg, showcasing the remarkable diversity of medicinal compounds produced by fungi. Indeed, the very nature of fungal life cycles contributes to this incredible chemical diversity. Fungi, being decomposers, constantly interact with a complex array of organic matter. This constant engagement in breaking down and utilizing diverse substrates has led to the evolution of an astonishing repertoire of enzymes and secondary metabolites, many of which possess potent medicinal properties.

One area of intense research focuses on the anti-cancer properties of certain fungal compounds. Polysaccharides, such as lentinan from shiitake mushrooms and polysaccharide-K from turkey tail mushrooms, have demonstrated promising immune-boosting effects, assisting the body in fighting cancerous cells. These compounds work by activating various components of the immune system, enhancing its ability to recognize and destroy tumor cells. Furthermore, research is exploring the potential of fungal metabolites to inhibit angiogenesis, the formation of new blood vessels that supply tumors with nutrients and oxygen, effectively starving the cancerous growth. This multifaceted approach to cancer treatment using fungal derivatives holds significant promise for developing more effective and less toxic therapies.

The search for novel antibiotics from fungal sources is also a crucial area of investigation. With the rise of antibiotic-resistant bacteria, the need for new drugs is more urgent than ever. Fungi, with their vast metabolic diversity, represent a rich and largely unexplored source of potential antibiotics. Researchers are tirelessly screening fungal extracts from diverse ecosystems, from soil samples to endophytic fungi living within plants, in the hunt for compounds capable of combating resistant strains. This relentless pursuit of new antimicrobial agents is vital for safeguarding human health in the face of evolving microbial threats.

Moving beyond direct medicinal applications, fungi also play a crucial role in the production of essential drugs through biotransformation. Fungi can modify existing drug molecules to improve their efficacy, reduce side effects, or create more easily absorbed forms. This biotransformation process harnesses the enzymatic machinery of fungi to perform specific chemical reactions, resulting in improved drug formulations. The ability of fungi to perform targeted chemical modifications makes them invaluable tools in pharmaceutical development, enabling the creation of more effective and patient-friendly medications.

Further exploration of the medicinal properties of mycelia extends to the realm of neurodegenerative diseases. Lion's mane mushroom, with its bioactive compounds like hericenones and erinacines, has shown promising results in promoting nerve growth factor (NGF) synthesis, a protein essential for the survival and function of nerve cells. This discovery holds potential for treating conditions like Alzheimer's and Parkinson's disease, where neuronal degeneration plays a central role. Research is ongoing to fully understand the mechanisms of action and optimize the therapeutic potential of these fungal compounds in addressing neurodegenerative disorders.

The medicinal benefits of mycelia extend beyond specific diseases to promote overall well-being. Many medicinal mushrooms are rich in antioxidants, compounds that protect cells from damage caused by free radicals, contributing to overall health and longevity. Moreover, certain fungi have demonstrated antiviral, anti-inflammatory, and immunomodulatory properties, supporting various aspects of immune function and overall wellness. The incorporation of these fungi into dietary practices or as supplements can contribute to a holistic approach to health maintenance.

The journey into the medicinal wonders of mycelia is an ongoing exploration. As research continues to unravel the complex chemical interactions within fungal networks, we can anticipate further groundbreaking discoveries and the development of novel therapies for a wide range of ailments. The future of medicine may well be rooted in the very ground we walk upon, within the intricate and largely unexplored world of fungal life. The ongoing quest to unlock the full medicinal potential of mycelia represents a powerful testament to the interconnectedness of life and the vital role of fungi in maintaining the health of our planet and its inhabitants.

6.5   Culinary Curiosities

The earthy scent of morels, the peppery kick of chanterelles, the delicate sweetness of oyster mushrooms—fungi have long graced our tables, providing not just sustenance but also a touch of the wild. Their culinary versatility is remarkable, offering textures from the meaty heft of king boletes to the ethereal crispness of enoki. Across cultures, culinary traditions have incorporated fungi into a diverse array of dishes, demonstrating the adaptability of these remarkable organisms. Consider the earthy, pungent truffles, prized delicacies that command exorbitant prices and are hunted with specially trained animals. Their unique aroma and flavor profile have captivated chefs and gourmands for centuries, showcasing the luxurious side of fungal cuisine.

Beyond the well-known edible mushrooms, a world of lesser-known fungal delicacies awaits the adventurous palate. In certain regions, for example, the wood ear mushroom, with its gelatinous texture, is a staple in soups and stir-fries. Its slightly chewy consistency and ability to absorb flavors make it a versatile ingredient in various culinary traditions. Similarly, the lion's mane mushroom, with its cascading, tooth-like appearance, offers a seafood-like flavor and texture, making it a popular vegetarian substitute for crab or lobster. Exploring these less-common varieties opens a window into the diverse flavors and textures the fungal kingdom offers.

However, the journey into the world of culinary mycology must be approached with caution and respect. Proper identification is paramount, as some fungi contain potent toxins that can cause severe illness or even death. Never consume a wild mushroom unless you are absolutely certain of its identity. Consulting with experienced foragers or mycologists is crucial, especially for beginners. Learning to distinguish edible species from their toxic look-alikes requires careful observation and a deep understanding of fungal morphology. The consequences of misidentification can be dire, emphasizing the need for careful and informed foraging practices.

Cultivating edible mushrooms at home provides a safer and more sustainable alternative to foraging in the wild. Species like oyster mushrooms, shiitake, and lion's mane can be grown on readily available substrates, such as logs, straw, or coffee grounds. This practice allows for greater control over the growing environment and eliminates the risk of misidentification. Home cultivation also offers the opportunity to appreciate the fascinating life cycle of these organisms, from the initial spawn to the fruiting body. The satisfaction of harvesting and consuming home-grown mushrooms adds another dimension to the culinary experience.

Furthermore, understanding the specific preparation methods for different mushroom varieties enhances both their flavor and safety. Some mushrooms, like morels, require thorough cooking to neutralize naturally occurring toxins. Others, such as button mushrooms, can be eaten raw or cooked, offering a range of culinary possibilities. Exploring various cooking techniques, from sautéing and grilling to pickling and fermenting, allows for the full expression of the unique flavors and textures of each species. Learning to properly prepare mushrooms unlocks their full culinary potential and ensures a safe and enjoyable dining experience.

The medicinal properties of certain fungi add another layer of intrigue to their culinary value. For centuries, traditional medicine systems have utilized fungi for their purported health benefits. Species like reishi and chaga mushrooms are revered for their immune-boosting properties and are often consumed in teas or tinctures. Modern research is beginning to validate some of these traditional uses, uncovering the complex chemical compounds that contribute to their medicinal effects. Incorporating these medicinal mushrooms into culinary creations offers a way to combine taste and wellness, blurring the lines between food and medicine.

Beyond their nutritional and medicinal value, fungi also offer a unique opportunity to connect with the natural world. Foraging for mushrooms encourages exploration of forests and fields, fostering a deeper appreciation for the intricate ecosystems in which these organisms thrive. The act of searching for, identifying, and harvesting wild mushrooms becomes a mindful practice, connecting us to the rhythms of nature and the hidden wonders beneath our feet. This connection to the natural world enriches the culinary experience, adding a layer of meaning and appreciation to the food we consume.

As we continue to explore the vast potential of the fungal kingdom, new culinary horizons beckon. From gourmet dishes to everyday meals, fungi offer a diverse and sustainable source of nourishment and flavor. By approaching the world of culinary mycology with respect, caution, and a thirst for knowledge, we can unlock the full potential of these fascinating organisms and enhance our appreciation for the interconnectedness of life on Earth. The symphony of flavors and textures awaiting discovery is a testament to the remarkable diversity and culinary versatility of the fungal kingdom.

7 Chapter 7: Reflections on Mycelia

The scent of damp earth still clings to my memory, a constant companion through-out this journey beneath the surface. Years spent tracing the delicate threads of mycelia across landscapes, from the shadowed forests of the Pacific Northwest to the arid expanses of the Sonoran Desert, have etched a profound respect for this hidden world. I recall vividly the first time I unearthed a network of rhizomorphs, thick cords of mycelia resembling plant roots, pulsing with a life force I hadn't an-ticipated. It was a moment of revelation, a glimpse into the intricate web that binds our planet together. The realization that beneath my feet, an entire universe thrived, unseen and largely unappreciated, changed the trajectory of my career. It shifted my focus from the solid rock beneath to the vibrant life it supported.

My initial geological training, with its emphasis on the slow dance of tectonic plates and the formation of minerals, provided a crucial foundation. It taught me to ob-serve, to question, to analyze the earth's story etched in stone. However, it was the discovery of the fungal realm that truly ignited my passion. The study of mycelia offered a different perspective, a closer look at the dynamic interplay of life and the earth's processes. I learned to recognize the subtle signs of fungal activity, the tell-tale patterns of decay and renewal, the intricate relationships between fungi and their environment. Suddenly, the landscape spoke a different language, a vibrant dialogue between the living and the non-living. The rigid lines of geological maps began to blur, replaced by the fluid, interconnected network of the fungal world.

One particularly striking experience occurred during fieldwork in the Cascade Mountains. I was investigating the impact of a recent wildfire on the local ecosystem. While surveying the charred remains of the forest floor, I stumbled upon an unexpected sight: a vibrant network of bright orange mycelia thriving amidst the devastation. This observation highlighted the resilience of fungi, their ability to not only survive but to actively participate in the recovery process. The fungi were breaking down the charred wood, releasing nutrients back into the soil, paving the way for new life to emerge. It was a powerful demonstration of the interconnectedness of nature, the way in which destruction and regeneration are intertwined. This moment solidified my belief in the critical role fungi play in maintaining ecological balance.

Over the years, my research has taken me to diverse environments, each revealing unique facets of the fungal world. I've explored the intricate symbiotic relationships between fungi and trees in old-growth forests, marveling at the intricate exchange of nutrients that sustains both partners. I've witnessed the remarkable ability of fungi to break down pollutants in contaminated soils, offering hope for bioremediation strategies. I've even delved into the fascinating world of endolithic fungi, those that thrive within rocks, pushing the boundaries of life's tenacity. Each discovery, each observation has reinforced the profound influence of mycelia on our planet's health.

This journey has been more than a scientific pursuit; it has been a personal transformation. Learning to see the world through the lens of mycelia has deepened my connection to the natural world. It has fostered a sense of humility and awe in the face of the earth's complexity. I've come to appreciate the intricate web of life that connects us all, the unseen forces that shape our environment. The quiet persistence of fungi, their ability to thrive in seemingly inhospitable conditions, has taught me valuable lessons about resilience and adaptation.

Looking forward, I recognize that our understanding of mycelia is still in its infancy. There are countless species yet to be discovered, countless mysteries yet to be unraveled. The ongoing quest to understand this hidden world is both exciting and daunting. It requires us to embrace interdisciplinary approaches, to collaborate across scientific boundaries, and to foster a deeper appreciation for the interconnectedness of all living things. As we continue to explore the melody of mycelia, we must also strive to protect this vital component of our planet's ecosystem. The future of our planet may well depend on our ability to understand and safeguard the hidden world beneath our feet. It is a responsibility we must embrace with both humility and determination.

7.1 Lessons Learned

The scent of damp earth still clings to my memories, a constant reminder of years spent crouched low to the ground, eyes scanning the forest floor. My journey into the world of mycelia has been a humbling one, a continuous process of unlearning and rediscovering. I've learned that true understanding comes not from imposing our human frameworks, but from listening to the subtle whispers of the earth it-self. The earth holds a language older than words, spoken through the intricate branching of hyphae and the silent, steady pulse of decomposition. It's a language I've spent a lifetime trying to decipher, and I've barely scratched the surface.

One of the most profound lessons has been the interconnectedness of all things. The mycelial network isn't simply a collection of individual strands; it's a living, breathing web that connects entire ecosystems. Nutrients flow through these hid-den channels, binding trees and fungi in a symbiotic dance. This realization shifted my perspective from viewing organisms in isolation to appreciating the intricate tapestry of relationships that sustain life on Earth. Every fallen leaf, every decaying log, becomes a vital part of this grand cycle, orchestrated by the unseen hand of the mycelium.

My geological training, initially focused on the solid structures of the earth, eventu-ally led me to appreciate the fluidity and dynamism of the subterranean world. I've observed how geological formations influence the spread of mycelial networks, cre-ating unique microhabitats that support specific fungal communities. A slight shift in soil pH, a subtle change in rock composition, can dramatically alter the fungal landscape. This interplay between the geological and the biological has been a con-stant source of fascination, reminding me of the intricate connections that shape our planet.

Patience has been another crucial lesson, cultivated through countless hours spent observing the slow, deliberate growth of fungi. Unlike the rapid changes we often witness in the world above, the mycelial realm operates on a different timescale. It requires a quiet attentiveness, a willingness to slow down and appreciate the subtle shifts occurring beneath our feet. The reward for this patience is witnessing the breathtaking intricacy of fungal growth, the unfolding of life in its most fundamental form.

I've learned to embrace the unexpected. Fieldwork rarely goes as planned, and the most valuable discoveries often arise from serendipitous encounters. A misplaced step revealing a hidden fungal colony, a sudden downpour uncovering a rare species – these unexpected moments have been pivotal in shaping my understanding of mycelia. They've reinforced the importance of staying open to new possibilities, of letting curiosity guide the way.

Perhaps the most humbling lesson has been the realization of how much we still don't know. The fungal kingdom is vast and largely unexplored, teeming with untold mysteries waiting to be unveiled. Each new discovery raises more questions, deepening the sense of awe and wonder that first drew me to this field. It's a constant reminder that the pursuit of knowledge is a lifelong journey, a continuous process of exploration and discovery.

Throughout my career, I've learned the importance of meticulous documentation. Detailed field notes, carefully preserved specimens, and precise mapping are essential for building a comprehensive understanding of mycelial networks. This attention to detail allows us to track changes over time, to discern patterns and connections that might otherwise be missed. It's a painstaking process, but one that is crucial for advancing our knowledge of the fungal kingdom.

I've also come to appreciate the power of collaboration. Working with researchers from diverse backgrounds – ecologists, botanists, geneticists – has enriched my understanding of mycelia in profound ways. Sharing knowledge and perspectives allows us to see the fungal world through different lenses, revealing hidden connections and fostering new avenues of inquiry. It's a testament to the collective power of human curiosity and the potential for interdisciplinary collaboration to unlock the secrets of the natural world.

Looking back, I realize that my journey into the world of mycelia has been a journey of self-discovery as well. It's taught me to appreciate the beauty of the unseen, the importance of patience and observation, and the interconnectedness of all living things. It's a journey I'm still on, and I look forward to the continued exploration of this hidden realm, guided by the whispers of the earth and the ongoing quest for understanding. The lessons learned are etched not just in my field notes, but in the very fabric of my being, shaping my perception of the world and my place within it. The earth beneath our feet holds a wealth of knowledge, waiting to be uncovered by those willing to listen. And as I continue this exploration, I am constantly reminded of the profound beauty and intricate complexity of the mycelial world, a hidden kingdom that connects us all.

7.2 The Ongoing Quest

The pursuit of understanding mycelial networks has been a thread woven through my entire career. It's a journey without a true destination, a path that continually unfolds, revealing new complexities and wonders with every expedition. I recall a specific dig in the Appalachian foothills, where the scent of damp earth mingled with the sweet aroma of decaying leaves. I unearthed a network of rhizomorphs, thick, cord-like structures of mycelia, radiating outwards like the spokes of a wheel. This discovery solidified for me the sheer power and influence these hidden organisms wield beneath our feet, shaping the very foundations of the forest ecosystem. This drive to uncover the secrets hidden beneath the soil fuels my ongoing quest. It's a fascination that transcends mere scientific curiosity; it's a deep-seated respect for the intricate web of life that connects us all.

From the boreal forests of Canada to the arid landscapes of the American Southwest, each environment presents unique challenges and rewards for the mycologist. The variability in soil composition, moisture levels, and vegetation dramatically impacts the fungal communities that thrive within. I've learned to adapt my methods, refining my approach with each new location. In the desert, I discovered the remarkable ability of certain fungi to survive in extreme conditions, forming symbiotic relationships with drought-tolerant plants. These resilient organisms revealed the adaptability and tenacity of life, pushing the boundaries of what I thought possible. The constant learning, the perpetual adaptation, is what makes this pursuit so captivating.

One aspect of my work that continues to fascinate me is the dynamic relationship between geology and mycology. The parent material, the bedrock from which soil is derived, plays a significant role in determining the types of fungi that can establish themselves in a particular area. The chemical composition of the rock, whether it's granite, limestone, or shale, influences the pH and mineral content of the soil, creating specific niches for different fungal species. I have observed how certain fungi are specifically adapted to calcareous soils, while others thrive in acidic environments. This interplay between the geological and biological worlds is a constant source of wonder. It emphasizes the interconnectedness of Earth's systems, reminding me that the study of fungi is inextricably linked to the study of the planet itself.

Beyond the scientific pursuit, I've come to appreciate the sheer artistry of fungal forms. The delicate tracery of a fungal network, the vibrant colors of a mushroom cap, the intricate architecture of a bracket fungus – these are expressions of nature's creativity. I've spent hours simply observing the subtle nuances of these organisms, sketching their forms in my field journal, capturing the ephemeral beauty that often goes unnoticed. These artistic endeavors provide a different lens through which to appreciate the fungal world, complementing the scientific analysis with a sense of awe and wonder.

My ongoing quest is not solely about scientific discovery; it's also about sharing the knowledge and fostering an appreciation for this hidden kingdom. I believe that understanding the importance of fungi is crucial for environmental stewardship. Fungi are essential decomposers, nutrient recyclers, and symbiotic partners to plants. They play a vital role in maintaining the health and balance of our ecosystems. By educating others about the importance of fungi, I hope to inspire a sense of responsibility and a desire to protect these often-overlooked organisms.

Looking ahead, I envision new avenues of exploration opening up, fueled by advancements in technology and an increasing awareness of the importance of fungal research. Metagenomics, the study of genetic material recovered directly from environmental samples, is revolutionizing our understanding of fungal diversity. This powerful tool allows us to identify and characterize fungi that are difficult or impossible to culture in the laboratory, unveiling a hidden world of microbial life. The potential for discovery is immense, promising new insights into the roles fungi play in ecosystems and their potential applications in biotechnology, medicine, and bioremediation.

The interconnectedness of the fungal world continues to inspire my research. Exploring the intricate networks of mycelia reveals the complex relationships between fungi, plants, and other organisms within an ecosystem. The mycorrhizal networks, the symbiotic partnerships between fungi and plant roots, are particularly fascinating. These underground highways facilitate the exchange of nutrients and information between plants, creating a complex web of communication that influences the health and resilience of the entire forest. Understanding these interactions is crucial for developing sustainable forestry practices and restoring degraded ecosystems.

This ongoing quest is more than a career; it's a calling. It's a pursuit driven by an insatiable curiosity to understand the hidden workings of the natural world. It's a journey that has taken me to remote corners of the globe, introduced me to a community of passionate researchers, and deepened my appreciation for the interconnectedness of life. And as I continue to explore the melody of mycelia, I am constantly reminded that the most profound discoveries often lie just beneath the surface, waiting to be unearthed.

7.3   A Love for the Earth

My boots, caked in the mud of a thousand different forests, feel heavy now, not with the weight of earth, but with the weight of years. I've walked across volcanic slopes still warm from their fiery birth, crawled through caves echoing with the whispers of millennia, and traced the faint lines of ancient glaciers etched onto the landscape. Each journey, each expedition, has deepened my understanding of the delicate, intricate tapestry that connects all life on this planet. And it is this interconnectedness, this symphony of existence, that brings me to the fungi, the mycelium, the very fabric that binds the soil beneath our feet.

This love for the earth, this reverence for the natural world, wasn't born overnight. It was cultivated, nurtured, through countless hours spent observing, questioning, and exploring. From the vibrant hues of a lichen clinging to a weathered rock face to the silent, steady growth of a mushroom pushing through the forest floor, each encounter has been a lesson, a whispered secret from the earth itself. These experiences have shaped not only my career as a geologist but also my very being, fostering a deep sense of responsibility to protect and preserve the wonders of our planet.

The earth, in all its complexity, is a vast and dynamic system. It is a system where the seemingly insignificant plays a vital role. The microscopic threads of mycelium, often hidden from view, are a perfect example. They weave through the soil, breaking down organic matter, releasing nutrients, and connecting plants in a vast, subterranean network. This network, this hidden world beneath our feet, is essential for the health and vitality of our ecosystems. It is a testament to the power of collaboration, the intricate dance of life that sustains our planet.

Consider the delicate balance of a forest ecosystem. The trees, reaching towards the sky, draw energy from the sun. Below, in the cool darkness of the soil, the mycelium works tirelessly, decomposing fallen leaves and branches, returning nutrients to the earth. These nutrients, then, are taken up by the trees, fueling their growth and ensuring the continuation of the cycle. This intricate interplay, this symbiotic relationship, is a testament to the interconnectedness of all living things.

My work as a field geologist has given me a unique perspective on this interconnectedness. By studying the earth's physical structure, its rocks, its soils, its landforms, I've come to appreciate the profound influence of geology on the distribution and diversity of fungal life. The composition of the bedrock, the slope of the land, the availability of water – all these factors play a role in shaping the fungal communities that thrive in a particular area. This interplay between geology and mycology, between the earth's physical structure and the life that it supports, is a source of endless fascination for me.

And what about the vast stretches of time, the geological epochs that have shaped the earth into the form we know today? The slow, relentless forces of erosion, the dramatic upheavals of volcanic eruptions, the creeping advance and retreat of glaciers – these processes have all left their mark on the landscape, influencing the evolution of life, including the fascinating kingdom of fungi. Understanding this deep time perspective, this vast historical context, is crucial for appreciating the resilience and adaptability of life on Earth.

The study of fungi, of mycelium, has taught me humility. It has shown me that even the smallest, most unassuming organisms can play a vital role in the grand scheme of things. It has reminded me that true understanding comes from careful observation, from a willingness to look beyond the surface, to delve into the hidden complexities of the natural world.

As I reflect on my journey, on the countless hours spent exploring the hidden wonders of our planet, I am filled with a profound sense of gratitude. Gratitude for the opportunity to witness the intricate beauty of the natural world. Gratitude for the lessons learned from the earth itself. And gratitude for the mycelium, the silent, unseen network that connects us all. It is a love for the earth, a deep respect for the delicate balance of life, that drives me forward, urging me to continue exploring, to continue learning, and to continue sharing the wonders of the fungal world with others. This planet, with all its complexities and challenges, is our home. It is our responsibility to protect it, to cherish it, and to pass on this love for the earth to future generations.

9 798348 393946